CREATIVE IDEAS
FOR SMALL GARDENS

in South Africa

CREATIVE IDEAS
FOR SMALL GARDENS
in South Africa

Jennifer Godbold-Simpson • Rod MacKenzie
Jocelyn Convery

First published in 1999 by
Struik Publishers (Pty) Ltd
(a member of Struik New Holland Publishing (Pty) Ltd)
Cornelis Struik House
80 McKenzie Street
Cape Town 8001

Reg. No.: 54/00965/07

ISBN 1 86872 323 2

Managing editor: Linda de Villiers
Editor: Brenda Brickman
Concept designer: Petal Palmer
Designer: Beverley Dodd
Illustrator: Daisy Kelly
Proofreader: Joy Clack

Reproduction by Hirt & Carter Cape (Pty) Ltd
Printed and bound by Craft Print (Pte) Ltd, Singapore

2 4 6 8 10 9 7 5 3 1

PHOTOGRAPHIC CREDITS

Shaen Adey/SIL: pp. 18 *(centre)*, 88; **Marianne Alexander:** Front cover *(top left, top centre, top right, centre right, bottom left, bottom right)*, spine, back cover *(left)*, title page, pp. 5, 12–13, 16, 17 *(left)*, 18 *(top)*, 19, 20, 28, 29, 34, 36, 38, 40, 43, 44, 46–47, 50, 51, 52, 58, 61, 63, 64, 66–67, 78, 79, 85, 86, 87, 89, 92–93, 94–95, 96–97, 99, 102, 104–105, 108–109, 114–115; **Elizabeth Whiting Assoc's:** pp. 74–75; **Nancy Gardiner:** Front cover *(centre left, bottom centre)*, back cover *(right)*, pp. 10, 15, 30, 33, 35, 37, 39, 48, 55, 57, 59, 70–71, 72–73, 80–81, 90, 100–101, 103, 110, 111, 113; **Ray Hudson:** Front cover *(centre)*, pp. 8, 41, 84, 112; **Anthony Johnson/SIL:** half title page, pp. 14, 49, 56, 68–69, 76–77, 98, 106–107; **Anneke Kearney:** pp. 18 *(bottom)*, 32, 54, 83; **Yvonne le Roux:** pp. 17 *(right)*, 42; **Gary Seole/***House & Leisure***:** p. 82; **Zelda Wahl:** p. 53.
SIL = Struik Image Library

C O N T E N T S

INTRODUCTION

From time immemorial gardens have served the same function: providing extra living space, a place to entertain and quiet refuge from the hustle and bustle of everyday life.

Throughout the ages man has delighted in the art of creating a beautiful garden, and the use of ornamental plants goes back to the earliest writings in existence. The Hanging Gardens of Babylon were one of the Seven Wonders of the Ancient World, and at the beginning of time, God Himself landscaped the paradise Garden of Eden.

Over the centuries the changes in garden style and size have largely reflected the changes that have affected mankind in general.

The 20th century particularly has seen massive changes in living styles and conditions. Where once garden styles reflected the European outlook, ideas for design have become far more international and often borrow from other cultures. Changes in architectural styles have also resulted in changes of garden style, with each architectural design demanding its own form of garden layout.

Although still divided up into two basic forms, namely the classic formal garden and the flowing, more natural informal garden, gardens with a special theme or feeling are popular. But regardless of style the main function of the modern garden is still to serve as an extention of living space.

New patterns in housing are continually emerging. Population densities around cities and towns have seen the sizes of building plots shrink. Once again, as in the earliest times, security is of prime importance. Living costs are high and so people are looking for easy-care gardens. But the change in the sizes of gardens has caused problems among home gardeners as many of the well-loved informal styles do not translate well into smaller areas, and the simple, formal designs of ancient times have again proved to be ideal for the small gardens of today.

1 DESIGNING YOUR GARDEN

While most people have an idea of what they would like their garden to look like, it is often difficult to get started. You may begin by planting according to a rough layout that you have in mind, only to find that the plants don't seem to grow well or they die off altogether. The first and most important aspect of design is to be practical, and to accept the limits of your situation. You might for example have visions of your home set in a delightful English-cottage type garden, with masses of different flowering perennials and roses over the front gate. On the other hand you might want a tropical jungle look. Both these garden themes are valid but impossible to create if the conditions aren't suitable for the necessary plant material. For this reason it is important to properly assess your site, study the changing climatic conditions in your garden, and prepare the soil for planting, before you decide which 'theme' you can apply to your small garden.

With these factors established, you can then move on and draw up plans, experimenting with different shapes and designs on paper before putting your plans into action.

PART I: PLANNING THE BASIC FRAMEWORK

ASSESSING THE SITE

Climate and micro-climate

Your garden is subjected to the climate of the area in which you live. If you work *with* this climate by using plants that are suited to the conditions, you are more than half-way to success. The one climatic factor that exerts the most influence on plant growth is temperature, especially night temperature and the incidence of frost. All plants have preferred growth temperature ranges, and to try to grow non-frost-hardy plants in cold regions is courting disaster. On the other hand there are many plants that need cold conditions to flourish, and are unhappy in very hot situations.

Within a garden you will always have areas that are more exposed or more sheltered than the general conditions. These are known as areas of micro-climate. Micro-climates are particularly important in small-space gardens where the layout of buildings and walls can change conditions considerably. A sunny garden surrounded by high walls will trap the heat and stay warmer much later into the evening than one where the walls and buildings cast a great deal of shade and allow in the minimum amount of sunshine. So regardless of prevailing general conditions you need to examine the micro-climate of every corner of your garden so that you can plan and plant accordingly.

In small spaces conditions change quickly. While it may seem that the whole area is the same, you will find spots, sometimes less than a metre apart, where conditions differ. This is often clearly seen in containerized plants. Matching pots on either side of a front door or a flight of steps may seemingly enjoy the same conditions, but if one receives only an hour or two more sun than the other, it will need more water.

Humidity, or the amount of water vapour in the atmosphere, tends to be misunderstood and often ignored by most gardeners. In large areas the general humidity of a region remains constant, but in small areas humidity can increase or decrease quite radically. Paved areas tend to react most markedly. In sunny, sheltered areas, both the walls and flooring add to the lack of humidity. Where you intend growing hot, dry-climate plants such as succulents and cacti, this dry atmosphere is ideal, but most other plants, especially northern-hemisphere perennials and sub-tropical plants, will suffer.

Another important aspect is the fact that a number of serious pests, in particular, red spider mite and white fly thrive almost out of control in warm conditions and low humidity.

IN THIS SMALL GARDEN TWO MICRO-CLIMATES ARE OPERATING. AGAINST THE WALL SUN-LOVING PLANTS ARE USED. IN CONTRAST, ACROSS THE PAVING A LARGE TREE PROVIDES A SHADY SPOT FOR MORE TENDER PLANTS.

Humidity cannot be increased by watering your plants more often. What you need to do is to water the surrounds, such as the paving and even the walls on a regular basis during hot, dry conditions.

A permanent source of water in the form of a pond or fountain is also an excellent way of maintaining relatively high humidity.

While hot, dry conditions are fairly easy to correct, many small gardens lean the other way and are cold and damp. This leads to fungal problems and the development of algae and mosses. To combat this, try to increase light and air circulation, and cut back on the watering.

While many small gardens are sheltered from the wind by high boundary walls, wind can still be an important factor.

One of the main problems is that the arrangement of walls and entrances often encourages the wind to swirl around the garden, and up and down the alleyways. Trellises, gates and carefully placed wind-resistant shrubs can all assist in the deflection of wind.

A PLEACHED HEDGE OF EUGENIAS MAKES A DIFFERENT AND EFFECTIVE COVER TO THIS PLAIN OUTSIDE WALL. IT ALSO LEAVES SPACE BELOW FOR PLANTING IF THE NEED ARISES.

Preparing the soil

Successful plant growth depends on the quality and formation of soil. There will be areas of any garden, new or established, where the natural profile of the soil has been left undisturbed. These areas will consist of a top surface of dead and decaying matter, followed by a layer of fairly enriched soil, with the more inert subsoil well below. Naturally the depth and the fertility of the important topsoil layer varies from place to place.

However, in cluster-house developments, building operations have usually resulted in layers of subsoil being brought to the surface. This, together with what is left of the topsoil, is used to fill in, level and finish off the garden areas. Builders' rubble very often finds its way into the soil. Together with heavy machinery and the to-ing and fro-ing of builders across the site, the soil tends to become very compacted, and so lacks structure.

Where you have fairly small areas of garden beds it may well be worth your while to remove this poor soil and to bring in a good mixture of soil and compost. Where this is not possible, the working in of thick layers of compost will help to rejuvenate the soil and improve its structure. In gardens where there are built-up beds, raised beds and wall boxes, it will be better to take out all the soil and fill the boxes with a good soil mix. One of the main advantages of a small garden is that it is relatively easy to improve the quality of the soil and to create special soil conditions to suit certain plants.

Along with poor soil conditions, building operations can also change the basic topography and drainage flow of an area. It is therefore important to ensure that the area does not become waterlogged. Extra drainage pipes and outlets may be necessary.

CHIPPED BARK SCATTERED BETWEEN WOODEN CIRCLES ADDS TEXTURE TO THE DESIGN. AS THE BARK DECAYS IT WILL IMPROVE THE QUALITY OF THE SOIL.

DESIGN PRINCIPLES

All gardens, regardless of their size, consist of various components. These range from things such as walls, driveways, paving, paths, statues and containers (non-living components), to lawns and all types of plant material (living components). Garden design is the arrangement of all these different components into an attractive and practical whole within the given space. While there are no hard and fast rules in garden design, there are some basic principles that apply to every garden. These are balance, unity and proportion, or scale.

Initially, getting to grips with these somewhat abstract principles can be very daunting. An easy way to do this is to visit as many gardens as possible, keeping an eye out for the use of balance, unity and proportion in each one. Don't restrict yourself to prize-winning or show gardens only, as poorly laid out gardens can also tell you a great deal. By the same token, you could use your existing garden and work out its strong or weak points, or you could study pictures of gardens in books and magazines.

TOPIARIED TREES THAT SURROUND A CENTRAL BED CREATE A BALANCED, FORMAL EFFECT, WHILE THE GRASSED WALKWAY, FLANKED BY HERBACEOUS BEDS, ADDS UNITY TO THE WHOLE.

Far left: A NARROW PASSAGE AT THE SIDE OF A HOUSE CAN BE TRANSFORMED INTO AN AREA OF INTEREST AND BEAUTY. HERE CONTRASTING PAVERS AND PLANTS BREAK THE STARKNESS OF THE PATH.
Left: AN UNUSUAL GROWTH OF VARIEGATED GERANIUMS: THESE PLANTS HAVE BEEN STAKED AND ARE TREATED LIKE TREES.

Balance

The first thing to look at is the impression the garden makes. Is there an overall arrangement of the various components or does the garden seem lop-sided, with too many things is one area and not enough in another? In other words, is there a pleasant balance of the components in the garden? While good balance is an intrinsical part of design, it is especially important in small-space gardens. If the garden is cluttered with too many plants and/or containers in one section, the whole area will look smaller than it is.

The way in which a garden is balanced also qualifies its style. A garden that, if there was an imaginary line drawn straight down the middle of it, reflects an exact replica on either side – in other words where the balance is symmetrical – is known as a *formal* garden. If the components are differently placed on either side, but the sizes and shapes of the components are similar, then the balance is asymmetrical, and the style is *informal*.

Unity

One of the main purposes of a garden is to serve as an extension of the home, and thereby provide extra living space. But this can often lead to a major design flaw: a lack of unity.

Unity can only be achieved if all the materials used in the garden complement each other and suit the style of the house. If a garden has too many different types and colours of brick paving for example, your eye will be drawn to these rather than to the overall layout. While in a large garden the use of very different kinds of materials is not a factor that becomes immediately noticeable, it is vital in a small space. A patio paved with reddish-yellow bricks, which is connected to a pathway of cement slabs, will immediately 'look' wrong, have a jarring effect on the viewer, and make the area seem smaller. The same applies to containers and their colours. Graceful gothic urns don't go with modern, geometric fibre-cement containers.

Proportion

Proportion refers to the way in which all the components in a garden relate to each other in size. A lack of proportion can be disguised in a large garden, but this is not the case in a small one. If, when you look at a garden, one component or a group of components jump out at you, overwhelming everything else, then you will know that the proportions are wrong.

When designing a garden, it is relatively easy to achieve proportion with non-living components. Living components, however, cannot be proportioned so easily, as plants not only grow taller but also wider. In a small-space garden, if the plants, especially trees and shrubs, are not choosen extremely carefully, they can quickly outgrow their alotted area, making the garden look small and cramped.

Other design principles

Balance, unity and proportion are amongst the most important design principles in a small garden. Others that need to be considered are form, texture, colour and contrast.

Every component, living or not, that is used in a garden has its own specific form, or size and shape. So it figures that each component – be it a plant or a container – has to be chosen not on its individual attributes or appearance, but for the way in which its form will fit in with the garden as a whole.

Texture refers to the surface pattern of the components. Wall surfaces for example can be rough or smooth.

Plants often look different against a smooth-surfaced white wall than they would against a rough wooden fence. Leaves can be shiny, or they can be matt, with a 'solid' surface. Too much of one type of texture will make the garden dull and uninteresting, while too many different textures will make a small garden look too busy.

Top: THIS TRELLIS SUCCESSFULLY MIMICS THE PATH'S PATTERN.
Centre: A COLOURFUL MIX OF FLOWERS IS ACCENTED BY THE SILVER-GREY LEAVES OF LAMB'S EARS.
Bottom: THE APEX OF A TRIANGLE OF BEGONIAS POINTS TO A BUSH OF PERENNIAL MALLOW.

Colour needs to be used with care in a small space. Soft, muted colours tend to make an area seem larger as they melt away from the eye, but strong colours come toward you, so the space seems smaller. High walls surrounding a small garden can be painted in soft, mellow colours so that they fade into the background.

Colour can also be used very effectively to provide contrast in a garden. By placing a white statue or a rich, golden-green conifer against a rather plain background, you will create a contrast of colour, which will act as a focal point and immediately draw the eye to that part of the garden.

Creating the illusion of space

Within the basic design principles and concepts, there are a number of simple yet effective ways of making a small space seem bigger. Most are based on misleading the eye by creating an illusion.

Wherever possible, 'borrow' space from your neighbours. Above and beyond your boundary wall there may be a pleasant view of shrubs and trees, even mountains. If you hide the stark outline of your walls or fences by allowing creepers to grow above the wall, your garden will appear to be part of the larger view.

Just as interior decorators use mirrors to make a small room seem larger, so can you use mirrors in strategic places in your small-space garden. A mirror will reflect part of your garden, giving you extra distance and perspective. A mirror can also be used to make a rather dull or dark part of the garden seem more interesting by reflecting a better area. And a flat expanse of water in a small pond will reflect light and so make a garden brighter while giving it the appearance of being larger than it is.

The eye can be drawn away from unsightly, high building walls by putting up a pergola, or a half gazebo. By making this feature very colourful and attractive your eye will be drawn in that direction, and the high walls will become an incidental backdrop rather than a dominant one.

In the small, walled courtyards of ancient Greece and Rome, three-dimensional frescoes – or trompe l'oeil – were painted on the walls, sometimes offering a 'view' through an archway in the wall. Even a simple doorway painted onto a wall will give the illusion of space, especially if there is a pathway leading toward it.

By the same token, a path that seems to lead to another section of the garden, even if this other section is non-existent, will lead the eye into and beyond the actual space.

Or you could 'divide' the garden into separate 'rooms', using screens and

THE CLEVER USE OF TRELLISES AND MIRRORS CREATES AN ILLUSION OF DEPTH AND SPACE.

hedges. Where space allows, each room could have a slightly different theme. As long as your screens are in proportion and don't begin to dominate the layout of your garden, they can be used to lead you in and around even the smallest area, making it feel considerably bigger.

To draw attention away from a narrow, paved area and to make it look bigger, place a large, glossy-leaved plant such as a citrus in a container at its edge. The eye will be drawn first to the container and plant, and then over and around it to the rest of the garden.

When your eye has to go over or around an object, whatever is beyond the object looks farther away. This illusion works in the same way as using large-leaved plants at the top end of the garden and light, small-leaved plants at the bottom end.

Changes in levels
The majority of small gardens tend to be flat. Even where there may have been a slope, developers usually fill it in. This is unfortunate as a downward change in level, especially in a small garden, can be a great asset, in that when ground slopes away from the main viewing area, it makes that area seem much larger.

Sunken gardens formed an important part of the layout of the formal gardens of old – an effective ploy that is easily incorporated into the small gardens of today. Where you have no natural change in levels, you should consider designing your garden to include one, or more if possible.

One of the easiest ways of incorporating a sunken level is to make it part of a paved area where the level change seems to be an integral part of the design, for example, by using steps. There are a number of other ways to create changes in levels and so bring a new dimension into the garden. A free-standing built-up pond or pool as a main feature could be used, as can raised beds.

Where your garden is on a natural slope, you will be able to use the topography of the site to enhance your overall layout. Your largest flat area could encompass a patio, and be as generous as possible. In small areas you may need a steep, vertical retaining wall to support the patio. If you don't want to build terraces and retaining walls, wooden decking can be used. Bear in mind that retaining walls and supports for wooden decking may need to be installed by an engineer.

When creating different levels in your garden, it is important not to allow the level changes to become too dominant; they should always be in proportion to your basic garden.

HERE THE USE OF DIFFERENT LEVELS HAS SUCCESSFULLY CREATED AN ILLUSION OF SPACE. LUSH FERNS AND SHRUBS TEMPER THE HARSHNESS OF THE DECK.

PART II:
DRAWING THE PLANS

Having thoroughly assessed your site and come to grips with its good and bad features, it is time to plan your garden. The best way to do this is to put everything down on paper. Some people may think that such careful planning is unnecessary for such a small area, but you will find that covering all the basic planning points from the beginning is to your best advantage – even for the smallest patch, be it a brand new site or developed garden that you wish to improve.

BASE PLAN

Begin with what is known as a base plan. In new developments each unit should have a site plan showing the way the house or unit is placed on the plot, as well as the position of the services such as water pipes, drains and underground cables. If you don't have a site plan, you will have to draw one up yourself. Your plan must be to scale and an easy scale to use is 1:100 (1 cm/1 in on paper equals 1 m/1 ft on the ground) for larger areas, or 1:50 (2 cm/2 in on paper equals 1 m/1 ft on the ground) for small areas such as balconies, courtyards and patios. Make four copies of the Base Plan, and number them.

BASE PLAN

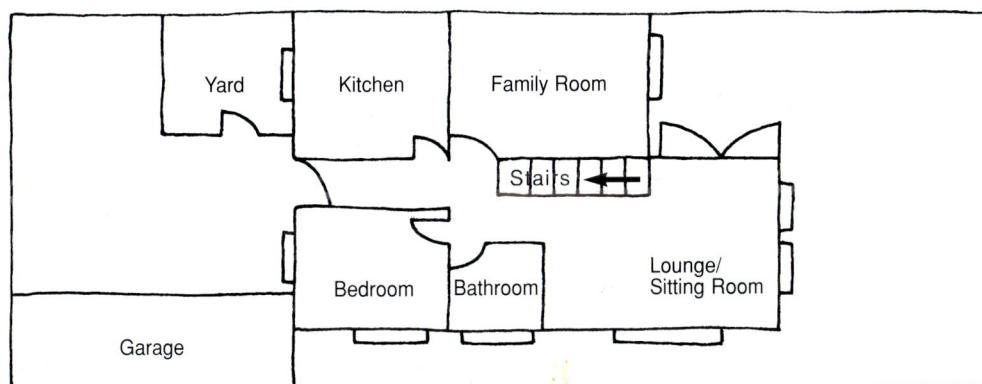

Yard | Kitchen | Family Room
Stairs
Bedroom | Bathroom | Lounge/ Sitting Room
Garage

PLAN NUMBER ONE

On your first copy of the Base Plan, add the following details (see *Diagram 1*):

- orientation to the compass

- direction of prevailing winds

- position of tap or taps

- location of service connections and outlets such as water pipes, sewers, manhole covers, down pipes, underground electricity or telephone cables, meter box, etc.

- gradients showing high and low points

- existing features such as pond, braai area, etc.

- any large plants, especially trees

- add windows and doors opening to the outside, and indicate the position of any good views, borrowed or otherwise, as well as any bad views that will need to be screened or minimized.

KEY

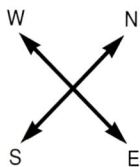

Existing tree

Tap

Manhole cover

Drain

DIAGRAM 1

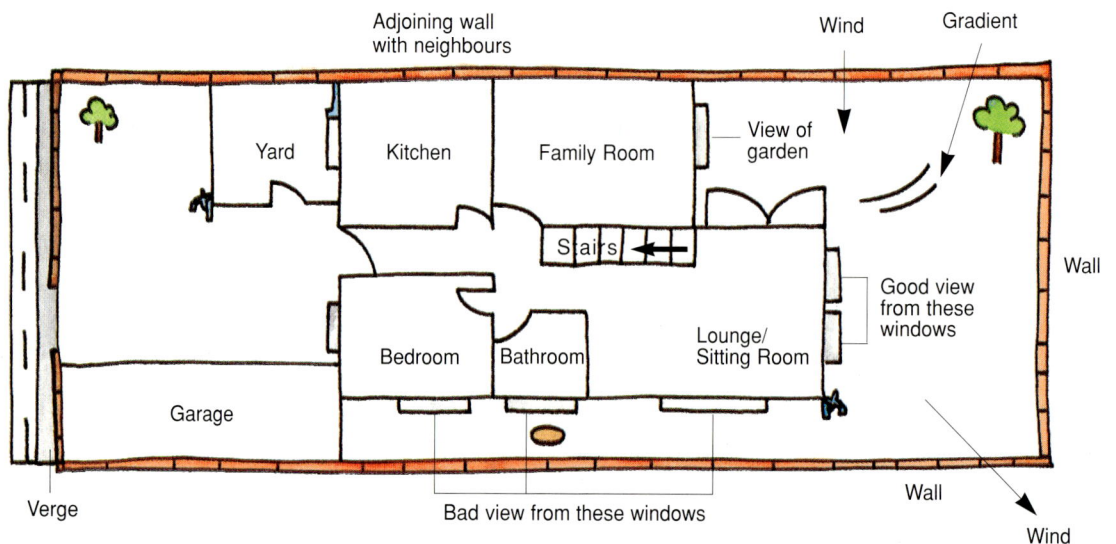

PLAN NUMBER TWO

On your second, clean copy of the Base Plan roughly draw in areas for specific activity (see *Diagram 2)*, for example:

- an entertainment area – usually the patio, but if space allows it could be another part of the garden as well

- the lawn area

- any hard surfaces such as paving, stone chips, etc.

- a small utilities area where you can keep soil, compost, tools and the like out of sight

- a play area for children (optional)

- a vegetable garden (optional).

Although it may seem unnecessary in small gardens to go into so much detail, you will find that knowing where and what your basic areas are will save you from having to find space for storage, etcetera after you have laid out the garden.

DIAGRAM 2

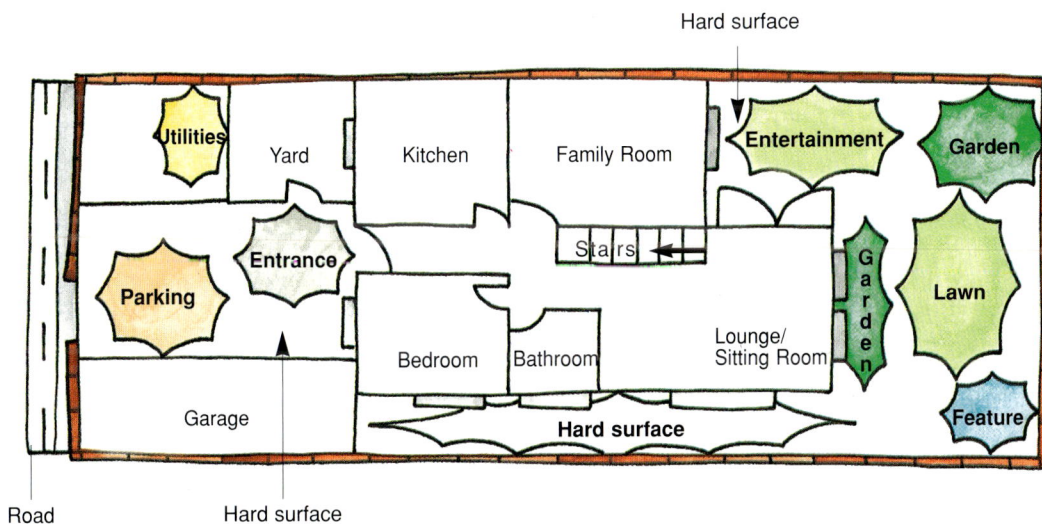

PLAN NUMBER THREE

The next step is to *examine* the shapes of the garden. Although it may appear at first glance that the shapes and lines, known as the garden pattern, of a really lovely garden have come about naturally, you will find on closer examination that this is not the case. A well-planned garden will have a specially chosen and consistent pattern that best makes good use of available space, and suits the style of the house or any large permanent features within the garden.

Geometric shapes form the basis of patterns in a small garden, and whether you decide to pattern your garden using circles, squares or rectangles, the beds, borders, paving and other hardscapes must all follow the same outline.

While there are a number of ways of evolving a pattern, using a guiding grid is a fairly simple and easy method that can tell you a lot about the use of space and how to achieve the right proportions within the garden. To this end it might be simpler to copy or transfer your Base Plan onto a page of graph paper.

On this third, fresh Base Plan, draw in a geometric shape, starting at the facade of your house, and repeat the shape until you fill the garden area with overlapping circles, or squares or rectangles. Try to follow the architectural proportions of the house in the garden (see *Diagrams 3a and 3b*). Here are some important factors to bear in mind:

- An *informal* garden is best served by a pattern of flowing curves, using full or half circles to create the lines. However, while curved patterns work well in larger areas, they can create a feeling of 'closeness' in a small garden, and this exercise will help you to determine whether or not your garden can accommodate such a style.

- Squares, rectangles, hexagons and triangles are *formal* geometric shapes and are ideal for small gardens and courtyards because they are themselves formal in shape. You can keep the plant material neat and tailored to suit these rigid lines by planting low-clipped hedges and topiary in a symmetrical layout, or you could opt for a contrasting, semi-formal look by using more flowing plants to soften the straight outlines of beds, borders and hard surfaces.

Note: In *Diagram 3a* I have used an informal layout in the front and back areas of the house. While it can still look attractive, you will notice how the space is diminished by the informal lines. I feel that the architectural shape of the house lends itself to a formal layout, and so have used this layout in *Diagram 3b*. I have carried the formal style through to the final stage (*Diagram 5*), and also offer an idea of what the final stage of the informal garden would be in *Diagram 5a*.

DIAGRAM 3A Informal Shapes

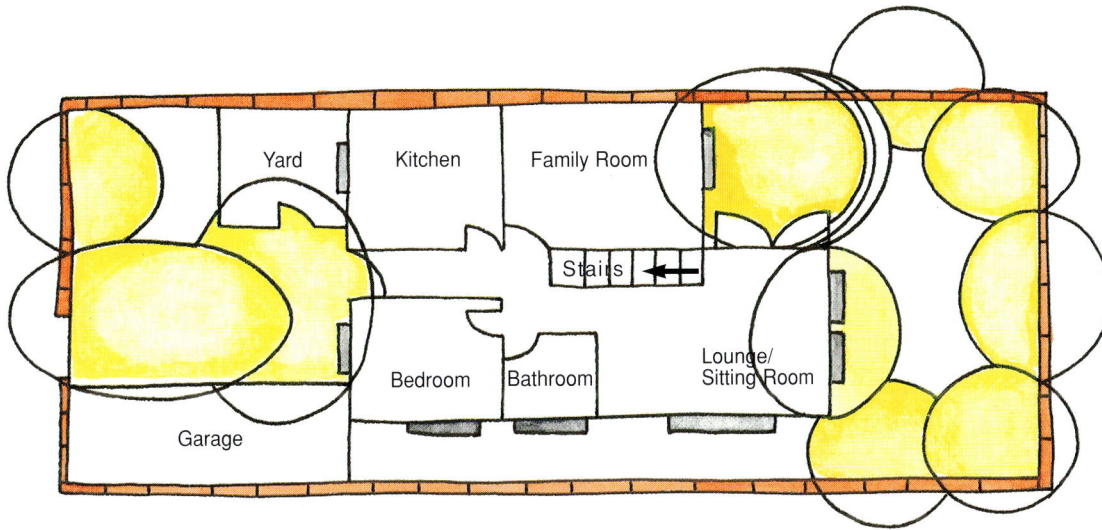

Yard

Kitchen

Family Room

Stairs

Bedroom

Bathroom

Lounge/
Sitting Room

Garage

DIAGRAM 3B Formal Shapes

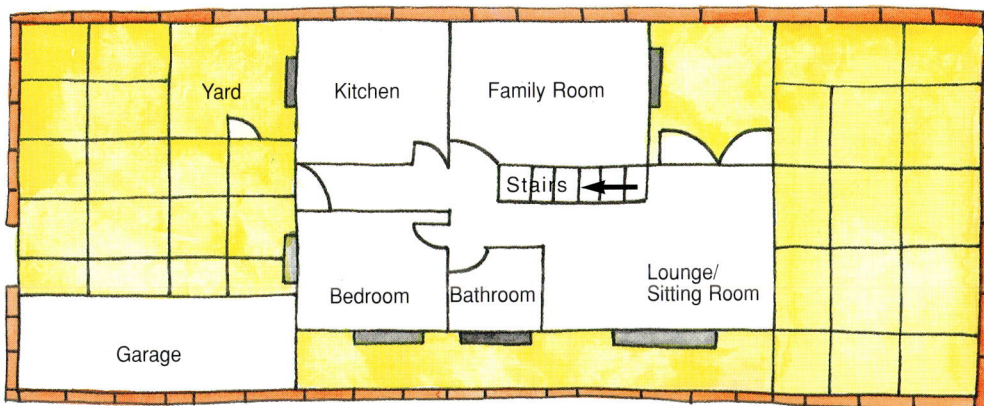

Yard

Kitchen

Family Room

Stairs

Bedroom

Bathroom

Lounge/
Sitting Room

Garage

PLAN NUMBER FOUR

Now transfer your Plan Number Two and Plan Number Three onto a fourth original Base Plan (see *Diagram 4*), adding detail and taking into account the assessment detailed on Plan Number One, making sure that your patterns and areas of activity have made provision for wind factors and that the view is not blocked, etcetera.

Here you can play around with the shapes, making them bigger or smaller, see how they can be used to give the plan definition, and how they can be used to influence flow in and around the garden from entrances or doorways.

Where you are remodeling an existing garden you may well find that you will have plants and features that simply do not fit in with the new layout. If the plants are really attractive, well-shaped or have some other unusual attribute, then it is worth trying to re-arrange the shapes so that they can be retained, but in a small garden it is often better to be ruthless and discard anything that is out of place. The same applies to features, such as a bird bath or statue – those that can be moved to a better position within the new plan should be, but those that can't should be removed.

KEY

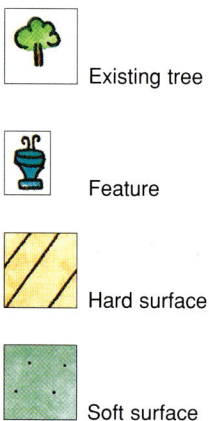

Existing tree

Feature

Hard surface

Soft surface

DIAGRAM 4

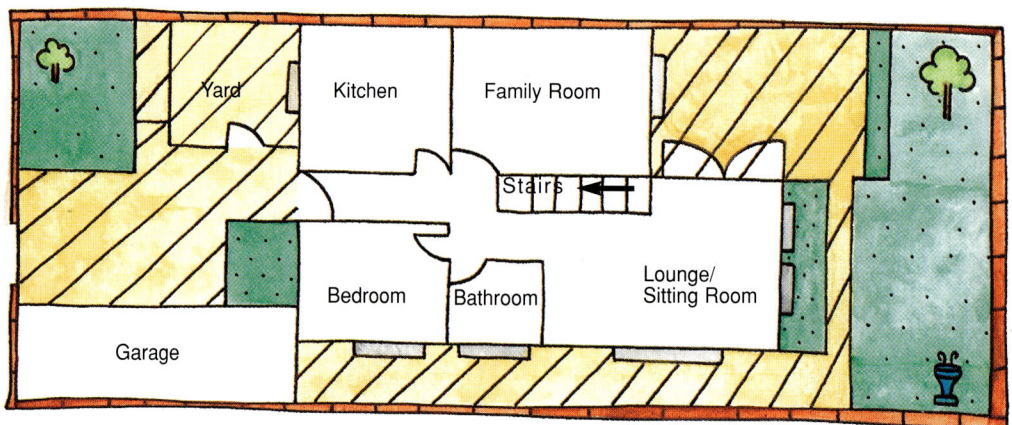

PLAN NUMBER FIVE

Once you are happy with Plan Number Four, go onto Plan Number Five. Block in the main shapes from Plan Number Four to indicate the details, including structures, paving and hardscapes, lawn areas, screens and any special features (see *Diagram 5*).

Diagram 5a will give you some idea of how your final plan would look if you had chosen to use informal shapes rather than formal.

DIAGRAM 5

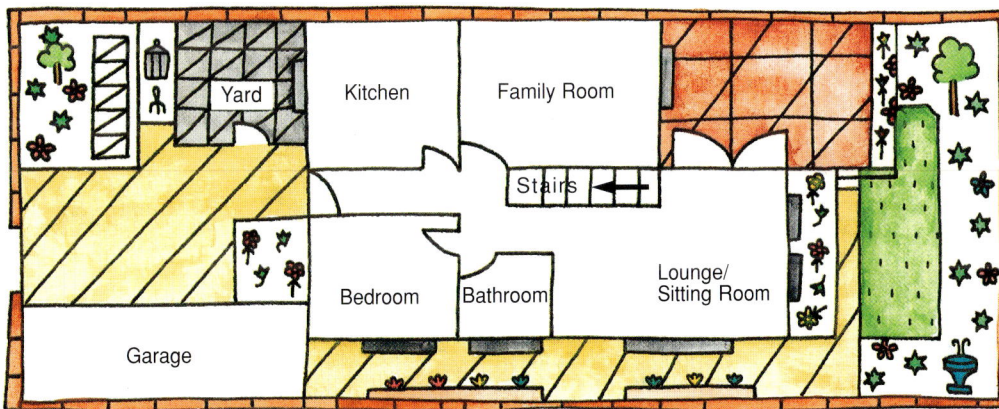

DIAGRAM 5A

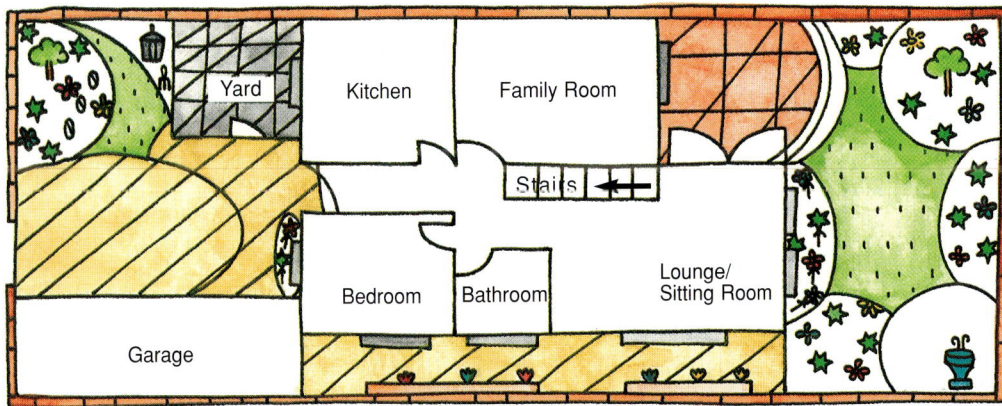

KEY

Compost/utilities

Slabs

Flower beds/ shrubbery

Lawn

Raised beds

Paving

Patio

Wall box

Water feature

Putting your plan into action

You will now have the makings of your final plan and you can begin making decisions about your plant material, colour schemes and all the finer details that make the plan unique to you.

If you begin by generalizing the plant material, you can easily become tied to specific plants and their needs, which could adversely affect the overall plan. Rather indicate the type of plants that would grow well, taking into account the climate, micro-climate and soil conditions. For example, medium-sized, sun-loving shrubs, a deciduous shade tree, dense evergreen shrubs, or shade plants. To help you finalize your plant material, you could well draw up a scale plan of individual planting areas – use a large scale for this, such as 1:50 or even 1:25. Try to visualize how the planting area would look in reality rather than as just a flat, two-dimensional diagram. Then, using all the relevant design principles, start to work out selections of different plants. Unless you have a great deal of in-depth knowledge of plants, it is best to go to your nearest nursery and place the various plants you would like to use together roughly in the positions they would be in your planting area. You will quickly see whether or not you have made good choices. For example you may well find you have too many similar leaved plants and not enough contrast in foliage shape and size.

Ideally when creating a new garden or when remodelling an old one, you should be able to do all your planting at once. This will give an immediate overall effect. Where the area is very small this may well be possible and in many instances more practical. But if time and money are limited, planting can be done in stages, and as long as you have done all the planning and have a good idea of what you want to achieve at the end of the day. In this way everything you add will fit in and not look like a sudden, rather out of place afterthought.

Opposite: THE FLOWERING CHAOS SEEN IN THIS CLASSIC COTTAGE GARDEN IS EYE-STOPPING. THE FLOWERS SEEM TO HOLD UP THE WALL AND THE TUMBLE OF CLIMBING ROSE COMPLETES THE PICTURE OF AN INFORMAL AND INVITING GARDEN.
Left: THE COMBINATION OF GREY FOLIAGE AND WHITE LILIES IS GENTLE AND CHARMING. LOW-MAINTENANCE GRAVEL REPLACES LAWN.

2 FEATURES

When the framework of hard surfaces and structures has been installed in your garden, or provision has been made for such installment at a future date, then you can turn your attention to the finishing touches. You might want a water feature and a rockery, or perhaps you envisage a plunge pool and a statue; maybe even containers, furniture, and a bird-feeder or bird bath?

It is important to bear in mind that a small area cannot accommodate too many competing features. Generally, only one special feature should set the character of the garden as a whole, while all other features should be subservient. In other words, you may have a water garden *and* a statue – as long as one is incidental, and the other a highlight; they should never be in competition with one another.

Generally speaking, features – especially statuary or water features – have more of a presence if they are raised above the ground level of your garden. They should always blend in with surrounding plant material, and with any hard surfaces on your property, such as walls, paving or gates.

PERGOLAS

In times past the Italians used the pergola as an attractive architectural feature in their gardens. These usually provided a shady interlude on a long, otherwise exposed pathway, and often served as a link between one area of the garden and another. Today, however, the pergola, attractively bedecked with climbing plants, has been adapted to serve our more conservative needs, and is often attached to the house itself – usually over a patio, affixed to a wall or even freestanding. In a small garden they are more popularly connected to the house and so become outdoor rooms, or an extension of the home, leaving you with the impression that the house is larger than it is, and offering a feeling of spaciousness.

Originally constructed from pillars with wooden cross-bars, today pergolas are constructed from a far greater range of materials. Some are roofed with Perspex (or other clear acrylic resin) sheeting to allow the warmth and light through while reducing the glare, and at the same time protecting the garden from wind. Others are fitted with retractable and adjustable canvas awnings, although these pergolas would create an unstable climate for plants, particularly if you leave the canvas drawn for weeks on end, and then suddenly expose the plants to full sun!

Whichever material you use, be sure to create a sense of unity and balance by using the same materials elsewhere in your garden, for example, the garden shed, dog-kennel and trellis walls. If you intend to completely cover the pergola in plants it would, of course, be unnecessary to use expensive material when a less costly alternative would do.

If your garden is a sun-trap, you may wish to cover your pergola with an evergreen flowering climber that will offer you shade all year round. Or, if you prefer to have shade in summer but enjoy the soft, warm sunlight in winter, a deciduous climber that sheds its leaves in the colder months would be more appropriate.

And, if it is privacy *and* shade that you are after, constructing a pergola will not only provide both of these factors almost instantly, but will not damage the walls or foundation of your house as a big tree might.

THE WOODEN BEAMS AND PLASTERED PILLARS OF THIS PERGOLA SUPPORT AN ABUNDANCE OF WISTERIAS. IN WINTER THIS CREEPER LOSES ITS LEAVES, ALLOWING FOR DAPPLED SHADE BELOW.

ARCHES AND ARBOURS

In a small garden arches can be used to great effect, as they can be set against a wall or hedge, or over a gate. An arbour can be used to frame a sculpture, a water feature, or perhaps a bench. These structures are generally freestanding, and can be used to connect one part of the garden to another, particularly where the garden moves to a different level or leads onto another 'room', thus enticing you to explore beyond its floral doorway.

While arches can be bought ready-made and are generally constructed from metal rods or wooden beams strong enough to support the climbers that will clothe them, a natural arch can be cut through a hedge or a trellis wall.

There is no denying that whatever form they take, arches create an alluring feature in the garden.

STRATEGICALLY PLACED, DELICATE WROUGHT-IRON ARCHES PRETTILY CLOTHED IN BLOOMING CLIMBERS WILL ENTICE VISITORS TO EXPLORE THIS ENIGMATIC GARDEN FURTHER.

WATER FEATURES

The magnetic charm and soothing presence of water in a garden can be applied in many ways. The melody created with each splash and drip, spray, trickle or flow of water is calming and peaceful.

A formal water feature is the most likely option in most small gardens, as informal features need a fair amount of space to look realistic.

A formal water feature looks best when raised above the ground, even if it is by just one brick. This not only creates another level in the garden, but immediately attracts attention. A raised water feature could consist of several tiers, which allow water to fall from one level to another; or it could simply be a flat, reflective surface, broken by a few reeds, or a single rock. Some have spouting fountains that shoot water high into the air, from where it falls down onto a flat surface, bringing it to life in a shimmering dance, and there are others still that consist of a raised ornament or statue that spouts water directly into a base.

The options are seemingly endless. However, the three most important aspects to remember when installing a formal water feature is that it should be in proportion and scale with the area it is in, it must fit snugly into the overall ground pattern, and the materials it is made from should be sympathetic to all those surrounding it.

There are three types of water plants, namely submersed types, which live completely under the water; floaters, which float on the surface with the roots suspended in the water; and types which root in the bottom of the pond.

Non-aquatic or marginal plants, as their name suggests, live on the periphery of water, especially on the banks of rivers and lakes where the soil is very wet to boggy. In the case of a formal garden where there is no bank, marginals may be planted nearby in containers, in order to expand the theme.

Opposite: A STILL LILY POND IS NICELY CONTRADICTED BY A STATUE OF TWO CHUBBY CHERUBIM, MAKING THIS A FUN FEATURE. THE HARSH EDGES OF THE POND ARE SOFTENED BY THE FOLIAGE AND FLOWERS PLANTED ALONG ITS EDGE.

Left: THIS ATTRACTIVE FOUNTAIN, WITH WATER DRIPPING GENTLY FROM THE UPPER LEVELS INTO THE BASIN BELOW, IS THE FOCUS OF THE GARDEN, AND EXUDES A SENSE OF CALM AND TRANQUILLITY.

WATER FEATURES ARE
EXTREMELY VERSATILE
AND CAN BE ENCOMPASSED
INTO VIRTUALLY ANY
GARDEN DESIGN.
Top: THE INFLUENCE
OF THE JAPANESE STYLE
IS SEEN HERE IN THE
SIMPLICITY OF THIS
KHOI POND.
Bottom left: A
DRAMATIC COMBINATION
OF WATER, COLOUR AND
CACTI IN A SMALL
TOWNHOUSE GARDEN.
Bottom right: THIS
CIRCULAR POND HAS A
CORRESPONDING PATH
OF GRAVEL THAT BREAKS
THE MONOTONY OF THE
RECTANGULAR SHAPE
OF THIS PLOT.

ALGAE

Algae is our biggest enemy and if it gets out of hand it can rapidly destroy a water feature. Algae needs fairly strong sunlight in order to survive, making shade a strong deterrent. It also thrives in water low on oxygen, and as water is oxygenated by movement, it is best to use a feature that requires a constant flow of water.

If you choose to have a water feature that is still, a variety of water plants, a few fish and some water snails will help to keep the algae levels low. Fish not only ensure that the water does not become a breeding ground for mosquitos, but they fertilize the water plants. The water plants oxygenate the water and provide shade, and snails eat the algae. Bear in mind that a water feature should be at least 30 centimetres deep and close to one metre by one metre in size in order to accommodate these algae deterrents.

BIRD-FEEDERS AND BATHS

Birds are not only entertaining, interesting and pretty, but they fill the air with their soft and beautiful notes. As if this isn't enough reason to attract them to your garden, they also make useful allies, keeping insect and worm populations under control. All the feathered visitors to your garden will keep a beady eye open for aphids, caterpillars and all the other creepy crawlies that would otherwise happily munch your plants.

Enticing birds into your garden requires no more effort than planting, for example, reeds, which make ideal nesting material, or plants that have flowers rich in nectar or those that bear edible berries. A winter feeding table would be a welcome sight to any of our feathered friends during the cold, lean months, as would a bird bath in the summer.

Unfortunately many bird feeders, and even some bird baths, are unattractive. More often than not the material and design of the feeding table or bird bath does not tie in with anything else in the garden, and the table (or bath) is often placed in an exposed area, drawing even more attention to its incongruity. It is important, therefore, to make sure that your bird bath or feeding table is of a compatible material and design so that it *complements* other facets of your garden. By the same token, it should be positioned in such a way that it is an incidental feature rather than the focal point of your garden.

A bird table or bath should always be near to shrubs or trees, preferably with the supporting pole obscured and the feeding platform just

visible above the shrubs or just below the tree's fringe. This not only increases the birds' feelings of security, but gives them an elevated focal point from where they can scout the area for meals, and at the same time keep a watchful eye on the cat!

The feeder should have low edges, to stop seed and other food from blowing away in the wind, and should preferably also have a drainage facility to prevent the table from becoming waterlogged and rotting the food, or, in the case of a wooden table, warping the wood.

Small bird feeders that can be hung from trees in the fashion of a hanging basket are also available.

The important thing to remember is that we should position the bird-feeder or bird bath in an area of the garden that is visible from within the house, so that we can observe the antics of our feathered friends without disturbing them.

A GARDEN SETTING DESIGNED TO ATTRACT A VARIETY OF BIRD LIFE HAS ALL THE NECESSARY ELEMENTS — A BIRD BATH SET AMIDST THE FLOWERS AND SHRUBBERY, AND A BIRD-FEEDER HANGING FROM A TREE.

GARDEN FURNITURE

A strategically placed, stylish bench or chair unfailingly beckons you, inviting you to sit, relax and enjoy your beautiful garden. Because permanent garden furniture is an artistic feature, it should be an integral part of the overall design of your garden, and blend both with the surrounds and the home.

When you select furniture for your garden, try to obtain a balance between style and comfort, so that seating is both functional and aesthetically pleasing.

Garden furniture comes in all shapes and sizes, and is constructed from many different materials. Plastic-coated or galvanized metal is the most common material, because it is durable and fairly easy to maintain. If you choose furniture in wrought-iron, remember that unless it is cushioned it will be uncomfortable, even if it looks very attractive. In coastal areas where rust and wind are prevalent, aluminium furniture is probably the most practical choice, however it can be very pricey.

Wooden furniture should be sealed to prevent rotting and should be of a good quality that will not warp if left permanently outdoors, while plastic is light and durable, and maintenance-free, and can usually be packed away if you don't want it as a permanent feature in the garden.

Furniture can be strategically placed to form a permanent feature in your garden, and to this end concrete and stone are the most suitable materials to use. As these materials are difficult to move around, make sure you are satisfied with their position before you place them permanently. Bear in mind too that furniture of stone and concrete is generally very bulky and may intimidate your small garden.

It doesn't matter whether your garden furniture is of classic, rustic, elegant or whimsical style, as long as it is 'inviting'.

Remember too that the positioning of furniture in your garden is as important as its style: views, privacy, surrounding fragrances and protection from the elements are all factors that, combined, will enhance the allure of the furniture.

A GARDEN BENCH DOES NOT HAVE TO BE PAINTED IN TRADITIONAL WHITE, OR STAINED BROWN, AS IS EVIDENT BY THIS BRILLIANT SAPPHIRE-BLUE BENCH, WHICH IS BOUND TO ATTRACT THE EYE, AND TO LURE VISITORS INTO SITTING AND ENJOYING THE BEAUTY THAT SURROUNDS IT.

HERE SCULPTURE AND FRUITED URNS HAVE BEEN CAREFULLY PLACED IN A TRIANGULAR SHAPE. THE EYE IS LED BETWEEN THE URNS TO THE FIGURE, AND THE LUXURIANT FOLIAGE SOFTENS THE EFFECT.

SCULPTURE

Gardening is an art form, and so a sculpture looks perfectly natural when placed in such a setting, but only when the scale of the model is in proportion and relation to its surroundings. Therefore, you should only consider the addition of sculpture to your garden once you have settled on a theme, and then only once the garden is reasonably mature, unless, of course, the sculpture determines the theme. In this case, remember that, as the garden matures the sculpture may diminish in scale and balance.

Sculpture can vary in size and subject, from a small frieze of singing birds to a group of life-sized statues, and can be amusing, serious, realistic or abstract in the viewers' eyes, and will influence the mood and atmosphere of your garden, sometimes profoundly so.

Basically, a piece of art should be weather resistant and look at home in a garden, whether it is placed in an incidental fashion that is unobtrusive and surprising, or it is the focal point of your theme.

Finding the right position for a sculpture is crucial to its success. The environment should complement the sculpture without detracting from its character, for example a soft frame of natural foliage will create unusual contrasts. Positioned under an arch and framed by cascading flowers and delicate metalwork, an intricate statue can create a striking impression. This same sculpture would look out of place alongside a bold, architectural plant. A mirror placed behind a sculpture can dramatically increase the overall effect.

A Japanese garden would be incomplete without a stone lantern, while a Mediterranean garden might incorporate a sculpture of say a dolphin, to round off its theme.

Statuary is not necessarily carved of stone, but may be sculpted into the branches of a large tree. In Denmark, a Forest Art Project was undertaken in the Marselisborg Forest. Here artists brought damaged trees back to life by sculpting images into massive bent or broken branches – with the aid of a chainsaw.

This form of 'organic sculpture' could be very attractive if you have a tree that forms a focal point in your garden, but has been bent over in gale and you are loathe to remove it.

Whatever shape it takes, be it classical or modern, unobtrusive or the focal point of your garden, a statue should always be in proportion to the size of the garden, and in scale with its surroundings.

TOPIARY

The age-old art of topiary, or foliage clipping, is too a form of sculpture, albeit one that has been modernized. Today, the endless training of trees or shrubs into artificial, geometrical, animal or decorative shapes is as easy as bending or moulding a metal or wire framework into the desired form, and growing a creeper over it. Traditional favourites for topiary through the ages have been hedge varieties such as common myrtle, yew, buxus (box), and the privet family. However, any small, dense-leaved shrub could be used. Fast-growing plants and ambitious designs can lead to endless clipping, so use the right plants and don't indulge in overly complex shapes.

Topiary can be used in most styles of garden – even those that are informal, where the sculpted shrubs will create a striking contrast and can be used to create a framework, containing the balance while at the same time defining a pattern. Topiary is especially effective in demarcating garden entrances, and can be practised in containers as well, although container topiary needs constant watering and feeding to keep it looking good, especially when it matures.

TOPIARY HAS BECOME POPULAR ONCE AGAIN. HERE A PRIVET HAS BEEN CLIPPED INTO A BIRD SHAPE. THE FORMAL OUTLINE IS IN STRIKING CONTRAST TO THE ALMOST WILD AND INFORMAL CLUSTER OF ROSES.

ROCKS AND ROCKERIES

A rock or even a few rocks can make an attractive feature on a flat surface. However, they should always be partially submerged to create the feeling that their presence is natural.

Building your own rockery in a small garden is no small feat, especially as the most attractive rockeries are those in gardens which already contain an area of natural rock.

However, that is not to say that you cannot build a rockery of your own. An important factor to keep in mind though is that a rockery in a *small* garden doesn't necessarily mean that you can only use *small* rocks. These tend to look like a mess that the builder left behind!

It is always preferable to use rocks of an irregular size, as uniformity of shape and weight can make the rockery appear contrived. A rockery should look as if the rocks have been exposed naturally by weathering. Rocks have water marks, or strata lines, that are caused by weathering, and when you position the rocks these lines should match up to form either a horizontal or a vertical pattern – whichever looks the most natural with the particular stone you use. To this end it is important to use only *one* kind of stone.

Rocks combined with plants usually look best when near water – or even in the water – or when they are on a raised slope (gradient) or mound.

When constructing the rockery, begin by staggering the rocks from the bottom of the slope upwards, with some leaning or resting upon others. (*Never* place the rocks in unnatural, concentric circles.) The idea is to create pockets for the plants which will keep the plants separated and, at the same time leave the rocks exposed. Try to picture what size the plants will be when they are mature – they shouldn't become so large that they obscure the rocks.

THE KEY TO USING ROCKS AND PEBBLES IS TO PLACE THEM IN AS NATURAL A WAY AS POSSIBLE, FOLLOWING THE FLOW OF THE GARDEN. THE SHARPLY POINTED LEAVES OF THESE PLANTS CONTRAST WELL WITH THE SOFT, ROUND STONES.

3 PLANTS AND PLANTING

Plants are the clothing, jewellery, and make-up that dress the garden and, by their arrangement, they provide the garden with mood, character and style.

While the temptation to overplant is very seductive, it should be held in check. Overplanting not only encourages insect and fungal invasions, but it also creates an impression of unkemptness.

As plants grow and develop, so they gradually alter the climate of the garden. If you plant a young tree for example, it will, as it grows, cast increasing amounts of shade, and inevitably provide shelter from the wind. Those sun-loving plants that you may have placed around the base of the young tree will no longer be appropriate as the climate beneath the tree will have changed and become more conducive to shade-loving plants.

You should always take your specific climatic conditions into account when choosing plants for your garden. To this end we have provided a list of examples of plant material suited to various conditions on pages 116–123 of this book.

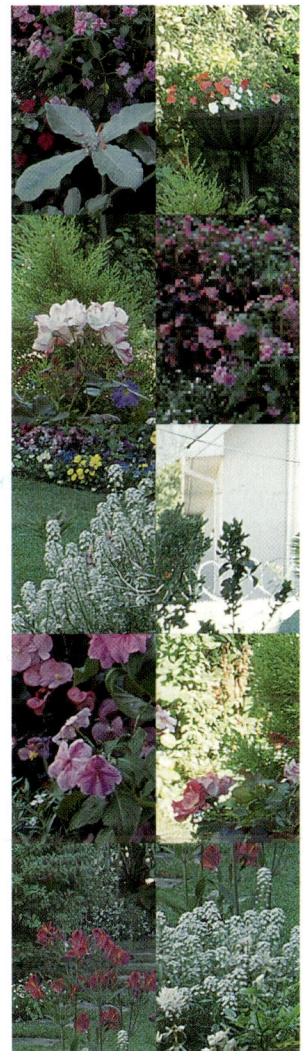

TREES

Many professional garden designers will start the planting layout by choosing a tree, or trees, first.

The tree is a dominant plant, largely because of its size, but even a small tree exerts a powerful influence over the final effect. As already mentioned, a tree can considerably alter the climate in the garden, and if you are going to have a tree or trees, you want the change to occur as rapidly as possible.

Because small gardens have become the norm rather than the exception, many smaller-growing varieties of trees have been introduced on the nursery market. That is not to say that a small garden should only have small trees. Often a large tree can be very effective in a small area. A tall house overlooking a small or narrow garden can be bought into scale by using tall, thin, pencil-shaped trees of which there are a number of varieties, including the conifer, cactus and palm families. These take up little space, don't require too much light, and will cast a scant shadow.

But remember that the tree you choose will set the tone and feel of the garden, and to some extent, all the plants that you incorporate will or should be influenced by your choice. If some other plant has priority, then it in turn would influence your choice of tree.

Be aware of the type of bark your tree will have, as this is often a strong feature, and be familiar with all its seasonal changes, particularly if it is a deciduous tree. If you do not have a specific tree in mind then try to imagine the shape, form and texture you would find most appealing can lift up paving or destroy boundary walls, while others will only tolerate specific plants around the base.

Some small trees, such as pear, peach and apple, are happy to be espaliered. Certain large-growing shrubs make excellent small trees when pruned to shape, and some trees can be stunted – if a small tree is what you really want. However, you should only resort to stunting in extreme cases. This is done by planting the desired tree in a strong container with very good drainage, and then planting the container, tree and all, into the ground.

Today there is a wide range of specially developed varieties which have a compact growth form. These are an ideal choice for a small garden. Most of the miniaturized trees are fruiting varieties such as apples, lemons and peaches.

and complementary to the setting of your garden, for example, a formally shaped tree such as a conifer, or a 'round' tree, such as a lemon. Find out if and when your tree flowers, and/or bears any berries or catkins. While a tree with bright red berries can look beautiful, it might not necessarily harmonise with your colour scheme; on top of that the falling berries may dye your pathway an interesting but unwanted purple, while simultaneously clogging up a water feature. At the same time, make sure you know about your trees' root system, as some roots

SHRUBS

Shrubs are long-living plants that branch from the ground. They vary greatly in height, width, shape, form, texture and colour. The majority of shrubs are evergreen, but you do find deciduous varieties. Most deciduous shrubs have spectacular bursts of colour in spring or early summer, accompanied by the arrival of their first, soft green leaves. The texture of the leaves transforms as they mature into their deep summer greens, which in turn give way to a richly coloured autumn cloak. Winter renders them naked, leaving us with only the bark and tracery of the shrub.

Many shrubs also enjoy fabulous displays of autumn or spring berry, which adds another dimension to seasonal textures, and some evergreens, such as conifers, have seasonal changes of leaf tone without dropping any leaves.

Like trees, when choosing your shrub you should find out if it is evergreen or deciduous, whether or not it flowers, bears berries or has changes in leaf colour. You will want to know if it is fussy about alkaline or acid conditions in the soil, if it requires particular care – it might require lots of water and feeding, or need to be pruned – what its root-system is like, how much light it prefers, whether it can bear salt-laden winds, and how child- or dog-proof it is.

In small gardens, where the emphasis is on year-round good looks, shrubs play an important role, and the way in which you arrange the shrubs is vital. Some shrubs – and here conifers spring to mind – have a dense mass, and a very formal shape, making them ideal for formal gardens, or as an incidental focal point in an informal garden. Formal shrubs are very useful for giving direction, and for separating one area from another, as they can produce a dramatic and effective contrast with informal plants. Interestingly, many formal shrubs do not flower, but they often make up for this with extraordinary seasonal textures.

There are shrubs that lend themselves to being clipped into different shapes, and this type of topiary is discussed on page 42.

Shrubs provide the three-dimensional pattern and form that we use to fill the vertical and horizontal space in our gardens. Because shrubs flower at different times of the year, and seldom for longer than two or three months of the year, it is a little difficult to synchronize the flowering to suit a mass colour theme. It is imperative, therefore, to pay attention to their shape, form and texture, before you consider what colour flowers they will bear.

Dark green shrubs should be planted intermittently with those of gentler tones, and you need to be cautious when introducing variegated plants, as over-use can be an eye-sore. Variegations of yellow, white and silver show up well in shady places or when situated amongst plants of deep hue.

There are a number of shrubs that can climb, trail and creep, and as such are happy to be espaliered or allowed to ramble through larger plants (see Climbing Plants on page 53).

Certain shrubs, such as yuccas, cacti and aloes, and many of the grasses, take on a formal, architectural shape. Generally an architectural plant should stand alone or be grouped with other, similar-shaped plants, and looks best against a pure backdrop, like a wall or the blue sky.

Generally speaking, if you want a formal effect from shrubs they should be planted in even numbers; for an informal effect, plant in uneven numbers.

Left: AN UNSTRUCTURED PATH LEADS THE EYE TOWARDS AN URN AND ITS LEAFY BACKDROP. THIS IS A CLEVER WAY IN WHICH TO HIGHLIGHT THE MIXED PLANTING OF SHRUBS ON THE RIGHT.

Right: THIS BORDER HAS A GOOD MIX OF FOLIAGE, COLOUR AND DIFFERENT SHAPED LEAVES, AND IS A GOOD EXAMPLE OF THE EFFECTIVE USE OF SHRUBS.

HEDGES

Hedges of trees or shrubs can be formal or informal, and provide privacy and shelter, define boundaries or demarcate areas within the garden, and can even be used in the art of topiary.

In a small garden, the ideal hedge can be kept narrow for purposes of space. Small, or 'dwarf' varieties can be used within the garden to separate certain areas. You can grow a suspended hedge with any tall-growing shrub where the stems are kept naked to the top of the wall, and the hedge is then allowed to grow 'down', so that it appears to grow from the top of the wall itself.

Different varieties of hedges require different levels of maintenance. Slow-growing varieties need cutting but twice a year. Other, faster-growing varieties would need more regular cutting – as much as twice a month during summer, but less often in winter. In a small garden a formal hedge should look good all year long, so the better option would be those that are dense, neat and evergreen.

Many hedges need to be watered as regularly as other plants in order to survive, and if they start dying because of lack of nutrients, the gaps would be impossible to fill when the hedge has reached its full height. Some hedges drain the surrounding soil, making it difficult to plant around its base, so it is important to find out about a hedge and its habits before you plant it, especially if it forms part of a bed or border.

If you use the hedge to demarcate an area, it should be tough-leaved and able to stand up to a constant flow of children or domestic animals. In coastal areas be sure to choose a hedge that can resist wind and salt-laden air.

Formal hedges

Formal hedges are those that we clip into a formal shape to create a living wall. The most suitable plants for formal hedges are those that have small leaves and remain compact and neat when cut, and are less prone to being woody.

Informal hedges

Informal hedges are rare in small gardens because they tend to take up a lot more space. The smaller types, or 'dwarf' hedges such as lavender or rosemary, however, can be used to mark boundaries or divide spaces, though these relatively short-lived shrubs may need to be replaced every five years or so.

Flowering shrubs used for informal hedges do need a trim once every now and then, but most types can be allowed to grow to maturity without ever requiring a snip.

Far left: THESE HEDGES FOLLOW THE LINES OF THE PATH, DEMARCATING THE FLOWERBED AND BRINGING ELEGANCE AND ORDER TO THE GARDEN. **Left:** AN INFORMAL HEDGE SITS NICELY BETWEEN A BED OF PLANTS AND FLAGSTONES, AND OFFSETS THE PRETTY SWEEP OF WHITE FLOWERS THAT ARE IN THE FOREGROUND.

VARIEGATED ORNAMENTAL
GRASS IS USED TO GREAT
EFFECT BETWEEN THE
RAILWAY SLEEPERS IN
THIS GARDEN. THE USE
OF GROUND COVERS CUTS
DOWN ON MAINTENANCE.

Ground covers are shallow-rooted, and so can grow under shrubs. This is very useful in containers, where they hold the soil down, provide a texture contrast, and often drape themselves over the containers, creating an informal look and concealing containers with no aesthetic appeal. Because of their shallow roots, they are often the first plants to indicate that the soil is dry and in need of some water. Most ground-cover plants are perfectly designed for holding up steep slopes, or for knitting a rockery surface together.

The term 'ground cover' implies that the plants grow absolutely flat, and while this is true of some types, most ground-cover plants actually grow to ankle-height. The virgorous types have a propensity to invade shorter shrubs, sometimes with delightful results, but more often than not this creates

GROUND COVERS

Ground covers clothe the ground with a vibrant, living carpet, often surviving where nought else could.

Some species can be used as lawn substitutes, though normally only in a symbolic fashion, as very few types can take much traffic. When a garden is newly planted the ground cover can quickly reduce a barren and bleak look, at the same time inhibiting the compulsion to overplant.

Ground covers suppress the spreading of weeds, and highlight shrubs and perennials, especially where the textures are in contrast.

The ground-cover family provides us with every conceivable leaf-form, texture and tone. Some miniature ornamental grasses, like the pitch black mondo grass, make wonderful ground covers.

Many scented varieties give off a perfume when trodden underfoot. Thyme, for example, can be planted between stepping stones in sunny places, while camomile or pennyroyal thrive in shady, cooler positions.

A large sweep of ground cover can successfully unify the garden. However, when using a number of different varieties of ground cover, bear in mind how their textures will harmonize. Growth patterns can differ tremendously, and it can be problematic to control fast-growing ground cover that has been interspersed with a slower-growing species, unless they are separated by a slab or small wall.

extra work as we battle to keep the various plants separated.

The conifer family has a few of these prostrate varieties, and their beauty lies in their disciplined shape, which they maintain with precious little fuss and bother. There are other very low-growing shrubs that can be used as ground cover.

If you use flowering ground covers make sure that they are sympathetic to your general colour scheme because they are often amongst the longest-flowering plants to be found in the garden.

Top: A PATCHWORK OF PAVING STONES AND LOW-GROWING ORNAMENTAL GRASS IS ORIGINAL AND PROVIDES A LOW-MAINTENANCE AREA.

Centre: ANOTHER CLEVER PLANTING OF GROUND COVER ALTERNATED WITH RAILWAY SLEEPERS.

Bottom: A DIAMOND PATTERN OF CONCRETE SLABS OUTLINED WITH SOFT GRASS IS AN EXCELLENT WAY OF MAKING THE CONCRETE BLEND INTO THE REST OF THE GARDEN.

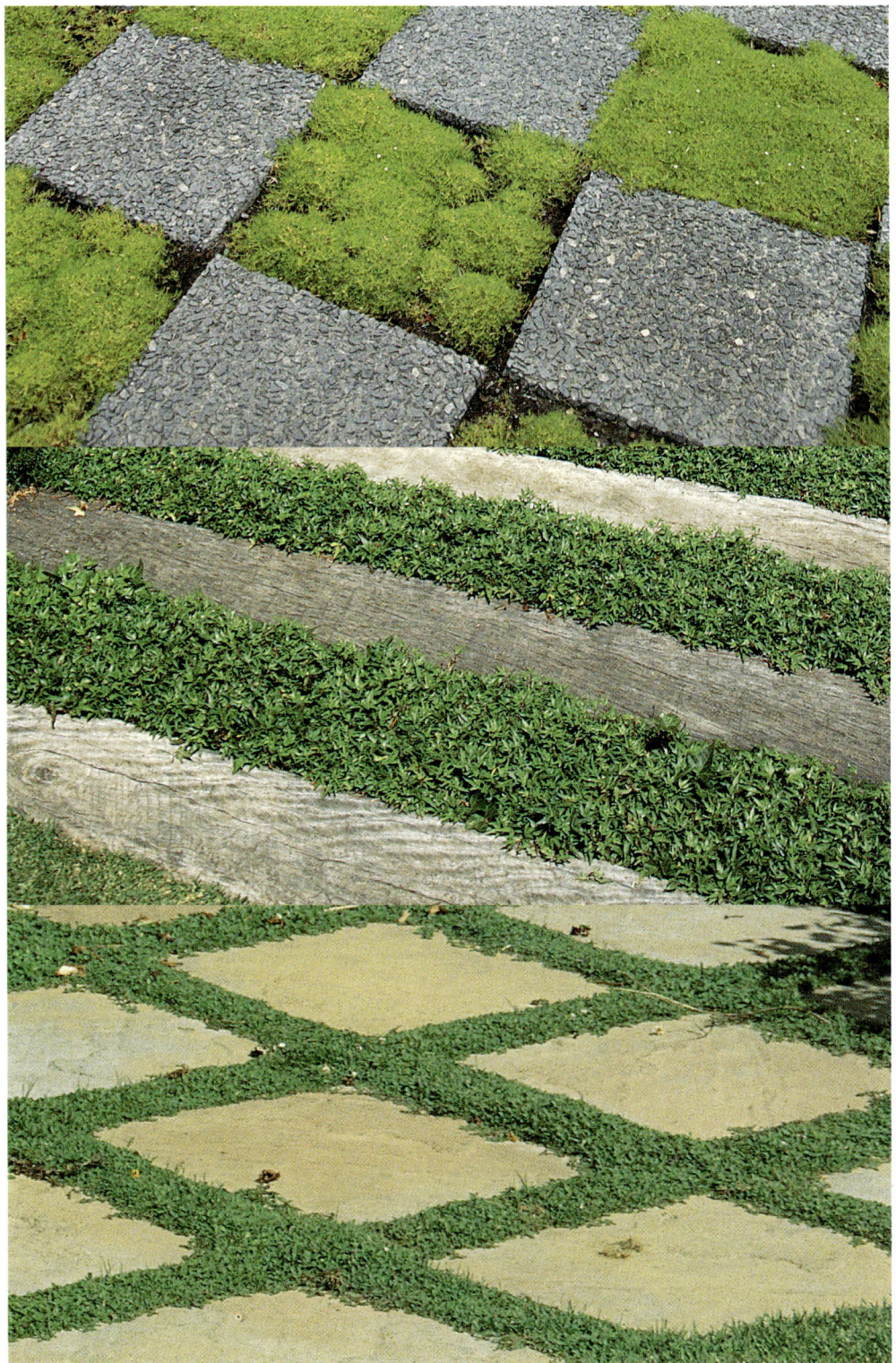

CLIMBERS

Climbing, rambling and creeping plants play a huge role in the confined space of a small garden as they take up little horizontal space while providing immense vertical coverage. Climbers are ideal for covering unsightly walls and fences with a waterfall of foliage and seasonal flowers.

Jasmines, honeysuckles and ivies are among the many climbers that can be trained to a desired shape and size. But avoid climbers with a rampant growth habit because they can swamp your garden.

Climbing plants have different ways of supporting themselves, and it is important to know how each variety accomplishes this.

Suckers

Climbers that support themselves with suckers, such as the ivy family, can attach themselves to almost any surface – with the exception of pre-cast walls, which tend to have a powdery surface. This problem can be overcome by stippling the wall with cement. These suckers, however, can cause terrible damage to plastered walls over the years, so it might be a better idea to use a fixed trellis to keep most of the suckers away from the wall. On stone walls they can do little harm and can basically be left to their own devices. Ivy tends to smother living trees, so be careful where you plant them.

Tendrils or twining stems

Many climbers have tendrils which wind around nearby objects, and in some varieties the petiole or leaf stem winds itself about branches for support. Others like common jasmine or honeysuckle have twining stems that wind their way about the host. These climbers need little training if you provide support in the form of a trellis or wires stranded across the wall, and need very little assistance before they rapidly find their own way.

Hosted

Some climbers merely grow through their host, and *lean* on them, so to speak. These include varieties that use their thorns as a means of support, such as roses – though they do need some training and support until their stems are strong.

THE EFFORT AND EXPENSE NEEDED TO BUILD A STRONG TRELLIS, AND THE PATIENCE REQUIRED WHILE WAITING FOR PLANTS TO MATURE SO THAT THEY CAN COVER AN UNSIGHTLY WALL IS AMPLY REWARDED IN TIME BY A SPECTACULAR SHOW OF ROSES.

ANNUALS AND PERENNIALS

Annuals and perennials can flower for long periods. While annuals live for a season, perennials can live for a number of years.

The fact that they don't live indefinitely, however, has some advantages. For one it means we can rotate the plants, and so enjoy many different flowers over a period of time.

Replacing annuals or perennials on a regular basis lessens the build-up of harmful insect life and soil diseases. And, of course, we can change our colour scheme regularly, constantly altering the hue of the garden to suit the seasons.

Annuals

The majority of annuals are summer-flowering, yet there are those that flower in winter and spring. Be that as it may, most annuals live for only one colourful season, flowering from infancy, and providing instant colour if purchased as seedlings; the majority of annuals reach their colour-climax after six to 10 weeks. There are certain annuals that, under the right conditions, can flower for up to six months.

Others, such as alyssum, are self-sowing and can be grown virtually throughout the year.

Annuals can be grown in large patches, or in small gardens they can be planted individually to fill nooks and crannies, or cracks and crevasses. They can even be planted in troughs or hanging baskets, or around the base of large container plants, providing splashes of seasonal colour wherever they may be desired.

Annuals are suited to virtually any conditions – from scorching heat to a shady bog. Most annuals grow to less than knee-height, but some, such as the sunflower and hollyhock, can attain heights of two to three metres.

Most annuals enjoy a well prepared soil with liberal doses of organic material, and thrive in good soil with only occasional feeding. As most annuals are shallow-rooted, however, these colourful plants usually need regular watering.

Bulbs that flower annually can also be used to ensure a continual splash of colour in your garden and can be used to fill the gaps between winter- and summer-flowering annuals.

Perennials

Perennials are non-woody plants. On the whole they are free-flowering and easy to maintain, although some need to be trimmed back once a year, and others may have to be lifted and divided once every two or three years as they multiply and become overcrowded.

There are two main types of perennial: those that become dormant during winter and those that are evergreen. The latter are well suited to a small garden, where even the tiniest barren spot can appear huge.

On average perennials are less than a metre tall, and this makes them an important intermediary between ground covers and shrubs. It pays to group together those that enjoy similar conditions, or there could be a disparity in growth and an increased risk of pestilence.

In a small garden perennials can also be planted individually – something that seldom works in a large garden – thus they make ideal plants for plugging unsightly gaps. Perennials are especially useful in a newly planted garden, where they may be used to temporarily fill the spaces that shrubs will eventually cover when mature. This also stems the inclination to overplant!

The huge and ever-increasing variety of perennials, including the many new dwarf varieties, will not only enliven your garden but provide you with colour, fragrance, aroma and cut flowers.

Opposite: THE PLANTING OF THIS HERBACEOUS BED HAS BEEN CAREFULLY THOUGHT OUT, WITH LARGE GROUPS OF THE SAME ANNUAL PLANTED TOGETHER SO THAT RIBBONS OF COLOUR CATCH THE EYE.

Below: PERENNIALS SHOULD FORM THE BACKBONE OF ANY MIXED BORDER, ESPECIALLY IN A SMALL GARDEN.

THE FLORIST'S GARDEN

There are those of us who wish to grow flowers in the garden to enhance the home. For the most part, cut flowers would consist mainly of seasonal annuals, perennials and bulbs.

But growing a garden for the vase employs not only the use of flowers, but also permanent plants that provide interesting foliage and brightly coloured berries – for fill and colour.

A number of shrubs and small trees with attractive variegated green and white foliage, or colour foliage such as grey, silver and plum can be used in flower arrangements. Some types bear ornamental berries and these are wonderful for winter arrangements when there are few flowers available. Holly and ivy are traditional favourites for the festive season. Perennials and grasses that have pointed leaves make a dramatic contrast to flowers and can all be used in the vase. Not many shrubs produce flowers suitable for the vase, with the exception of roses. Because the most popular cut flowers are the ones with long stems, the wind is a flower's worst enemy. Foliage plants should be spaced around them so as to provide shelter for your flowering annuals, perennials and bulbs.

A MIXED PLANTING OF COLOURFUL ROSES AND PERENNIALS AND TEXTURED FOLIAGE PLANTS WILL, WHEN CUT AND COMBINED, ATTRACTIVELY FILL A FLORIST'S VASE.

SCENT IN THE GARDEN

The perfume provided by plants must be one of the most delightful and alluring aspects of a garden, and when selecting our plants it should always be of interest to us what contribution they might make to the overall scent of the garden.

The scent given off by the leaves of plants is considered to be an aroma. Some leaves release an aroma when the plant is wet, and some respond to the heat of the sun, but they can also emit an aroma when they are touched or bruised,

so positioning them correctly is of paramount importance. Flowers usually give off a fragrance. As the aromas and fragrances blend, they should provide a pleasing perfume. In a small garden it is important not to allow a single aroma to become overpowering, but rather to create a subtle blend of pleasant scents.

Annuals, perennials and bulbs

In the fragrance department there is no shortage of scent. Using annuals and bulbs alone, you could ensure a pleasant fragrance in your garden for most of the year.

These include bulbs such as freesias, hyacinth and narcissus. The graceful lily family has a range of heavenly fragrances to offer us. St Joseph's lily and *Lillium regale* are two of the most popular and easiest to grow, both of which flower from early to mid-summer, and the golden rayed lily (*L. auratum*), which flowers from mid-summer deep into the autumn months.

Sweet-scented annuals include sweet peas, alyssum, stocks, mignonette and flowering tobacco.

Perennials noted for their fragrance include sweet violets and garden pinks.

Shrubs

There is a wide range of scented flowering shrubs. Mock orange, yesterday-today-and-tomorrow, winter sweet, gardenia, sweet-pea bush and orange jasmine are all well known for their fragrance, and no scented garden should be without roses, of which some have a more outstanding perfume than others.

For gardens in the warm, frost-free regions, a moonflower (*Datura cornigera*) releases its heady fragrance in the evenings and at night. Another highly scented frost-free shrubs is the frangipani. This shrub can actually become a small tree, but if space does not allow, it can be stunted in a container and kept as a shrub. The frangipani flowers from late summer into winter, and it is one of the most powerfully scented plants to be found, so be careful where you position it. It is a deciduous shrub, and winter nakedness reduces it to a dramatic architectural shape, with a soft, shiny blue grey bark.

Of the larger shrubs that offer a scent, there are few to rival members of the citrus family. Many of them make excellent container specimens, including the profusely flowering kumquat and calamondin.

There are a number of large and small shrubs that release aromas when sun-kissed or caressed. Few can rival the scented geraniums, or rosemary and lavender. If possible these should be positioned in such a way that they may be brushed against by passing traffic.

Ground covers

There are a number of aromatic ground covers, especially among the low-growing herbs, which are suited to either sun or shade. These can be grown along or between pathways, which they are inclined to invade. Here the touch of passing traffic will release their soothing aromas.

Trees

In a limited space, try to plant a small tree that might have a combination of aromatic leaves and fragrant blossoms. These could include citrus varieties, particularly orange or lemon.

The Australian frangipani *(Hymnosporum flavum)* is a small loose-leaved tree – ideal for a small garden – that reaches a height of about four metres tall, with a smallish crown. Pale yellow flowers appear during most of summer to give of their sweet perfume.

Climbers

The climber family has many fragrances to offer and few are better for the small garden than the well-known honeysuckle family, which is tough and versatile. These can grow in a fair amount of shade, but the more the shade the less flower and fragrance you are likely to enjoy. Many types of jasmine are noted for their perfume and make a good choice for a small garden, as they do exceedingly well on a trellis or fence. There are many varieties of climbing roses which are strongly scented, and can provide you with beauty, fragrance and at the same time take up very little space.

A WINDOW FRAMES THE SCENTED HERB GARDEN BEYOND. THE HEAT OF THE SUN RELEASES THE SCENT OF THESE AROMATIC PLANTS, AND THE BREEZE CARRIES THE SMELL OF THE HERBS INTO THE HOUSE.

THE SMALL KITCHEN GARDEN

Many a city dweller has a bit of the farmer flowing through the veins, with a yearning to grow plants that can be harvested for the kitchen. It's a treat and a thrill to go into your own garden and pick a sprig of fresh thyme or rosemary, a few pinches of dew-laden parsley, a couple of crisp lettuce and spinach leaves, and a handful of tangy radish. What is more, the miniature farm can be a feast to the eyes, with a wonderful array of shapes and textures, tastes, fragrance and flowers. Vegetables and herbs make very good companions aesthetically, and small annuals such as marigolds can be incorporated in the garden to repel insects and add splashes of pretty, long-lasting colour.

A kitchen garden can be grown in a barrel, a raised bed or on open ground, as long as it has more than seven hours of sun a day and not too much wind. The soil must be composted, at least 30 centimetres deep, and well turned and aerated. Plants such as chives, spring onions and carrots should be planted in groups to make an impact. Larger plants such as chillies, aubergines and peppers can be planted individually, as can most of the herbs.

If the 'farm' is bigger then a double bed, then it should be given access pathways that make an attractive ground pattern. This framework strengthens the plant groupings, and elevates the ensemble as a feature. The pathway could be a single row of bricks laid sideways. These look better when embedded in the earth and you could use the same material to make a frame. A pathway system helps to prevent the earth from hardening or becoming compact, which is the one thing vegetables loath – if you lightly break the earth between your vegetables now and then their performance will increase dramatically.

The back or centre of the larger kitchen garden could incorporate a small feature, like a sun-dial or a bay leaf tree in a clay pot.

A small kitchen garden that combines herbs, salads, vegetables, and annual flowering plants can be attractive throughout the year, as only one or two need replacing at a time. For example, different vegetables will mature at different rates, in other words the entire bed will not be harvested simultaneously, so when the carrots have been harvested they may be replaced with radish.

WHAT CAN BE MORE SATISFYING THAN NIPPING A SPRIG OF FRESH PARSLEY OR ROSEMARY FROM YOUR VERY OWN KITCHEN GARDEN? THIS SMALL RECTANGULAR SPACE HAS BEEN TURNED INTO A REGULAR GARDEN OF 'AT YOUR FINGERTIPS' CULINARY DELIGHTS.

GARDENING
IN THE SHADE

Every garden has an area of shade and this is usually welcome as it affords the opportunity to use different plants, and to create a separate theme within the style of the garden.

There are different degrees of shade, and it is essential to try to discern the nature and amount of shade that your garden receives, in order to get the maximum performance from your plants. A garden that receives less than three hours' early morning sun, or less than three hours' late afternoon sun can be considered to be a shade garden, as can a garden that receives less than two hours' midday sun. Shade can be light, or gentle, when sunlight filters though the trees, or it can be heavy, or solid, when created by buildings and walls. A half-an-hours' extra sun or bright light can make all the

difference between a plant that flowers well and one that does not. However, some small gardens are in complete shade, and this presents a challenge.

In order to create extra light in a shade garden, you should make as many of the hard surfaces – such as pathways, walls and containers – a light colour or tone, as this will reflect natural light and have the added effect of making a small area seem larger.

The majority of shade-loving plants originate from either temperate forests, or from tropical jungles, and so it is that gardeners in temperate regions would make use of plants from the forests, and those who garden in warm to humid conditions would avail themselves of the jungle-type plants. A fortunate few live in regions where it is possible to make use of both forest and jungle plants, and there are some plants such as impatiens, hydrangeas and certain tree ferns that can be accommodated in both climates – though such plants might be used in different ways.

Shade-loving plants tend to have dramatic leaves due to the adaptations they have

made to catch a limited amount of light. Many have developed large, ornate leaves for this purpose, such as the delicious monster (*Monstera delisiosa*) and *Gunnera manicata* while others, such as azaleas and most ferns, have developed closely packed, small leaves for the same reason. These dramatic textures and forms go some way to compensate for the fact that many shade-loving plants have insignificant or sparse and short-lived flowers. Another factor that is important to remember is that most shade-lovers from the temperate forests, such as camellias, rhododendrons and fuchsias prefer acidic soil – and so it could be worth your while to have your soil analysed.

Although forests and jungles can be perpetually wet, the drainage in these areas is for the most part excellent, largely due to the enormous number of roots in the ground.

In urban areas the shade garden is likely to be either very dry – because it is sheltered by buildings, or very wet – because of a lack of decent drainage. In these instances the soil can be made acidic and more

porous with liberal additions of acid compost.

Shade plants have a lushness about them that inclines us to arrange them in an informal, forest fashion, but they can be planted in a more formal pattern by arranging them in neat sweeps and groupings.

In shade areas that receive fairly strong light or at least one or two hours of direct sun, it is not too difficult to find suitable plants. It is those areas of dense, permanent shade that often prove the most difficult. It is important that an area of solid shade is not overcrowded with plants, as this can only exacerbate the lack of light situation. Plants in deep shade must not only be able to attain their proper size and form, but should also be virtually freestanding so as to be visible as entities. To facilitate this effect, alternate a tall plant with a short, compact shrub, then a low ground cover, and then a tall plant again. Or create divisions between groupings with patches of stone, or a garden ornament of some sort.

Remember that in the shade leaf tone assumes extra importance, and there should be subtle to dramatic contrast between neighbouring plants to ensure that they all retain their identity, as plants with a similar leaf tone tend to merge. In other words, try to have a selection of contrasting leaf colour and texture, such as variegated leaves for colour, and glossy leaves to reflect the light.

Trees and larger shrubs

Small trees suited to deep shade are not plentiful, and many that are, such as the stunning dwarf maples, are very slow growing. These are often more impressive when grown in containers. The camellia family has a number of compact specimens. However, the lower branches need to be removed to create a tree shape, and while they will flower less profusely in deep shade, they do have an attractive, glossy foliage.

Members of the holly family provide a number of different tall-growing shrubs that can be made into trees, and here the types with variegations are particularly effective as they show up so well in dark places. The tree-like shrub *Fatsia japonica* has large, pendulous, soft green leaves with a sheen, and in summer it sports sprays of green puff-ball flowers. In frost-free regions, most varieties of variegated *Coprosma* grow well in the shade, and can be treed, as they respond very well to shaping. Weeping figs are very pretty and also grow well in shaded, warmer conditions.

Medium to small shrubs

Eleagnus pungens is a compact species of shrub that is available in various parts of the world and is tough, easy to grow, and usually pest free.

Also suitable are various types of euonymus, the Indian hawthorn (*Raphiolepis indica*) and the fragrant gardenias of which there are a few varieties, including a dwarf type. Gardenias also make an excellent container plant.

There are over 10 000 known species in the fern

A SUCCESSFUL GARDEN HAS BEEN MADE HERE BY WORKING WITH THE DEEP SHADE TO CREATE AN AIR OF MYSTERY. THE STRAIGHT LINES OF BAMBOO ARE A SYMMETRICAL CONTRAST TO THE CURVED LAYOUT OF THE CONCRETE PATH.

family, and these range in size from minute (some types look more like a moss than a fern), to gigantic, with some tree ferns attaining a height of 17 metres. If conditions are reasonable, then ferns tend to be one of the easiest of plants to grow, needing little more care than the removal of dead fronds once a year. Ferns of different sorts blend well together and make very pleasant compositions.

Climbers

There are no less than 20 varieties of ivy and all of them do very well in shade. Other shade-loving climbers include star jasmine, and members of the Hoya and Pandorea families (in warmer climates). Honeysuckle will grow in the shade, but the flowers are likely to be sparse.

Ground covers

There are many different shade-loving ground covers with attractive leaves and even pretty flowers, but the choice will depend entirely on your climate. These include periwinkle, dead nettle, bugle, spurflower and *Pachysandra* spp.

Annuals and perennials

Plantain lily, various types of bamboo, dwarf agapanthus, bellflowers, spurflowers and *Bergenia* spp. all provide a number of perennial species that are suited to growth in shadey spots. Hyacinths in white, pink, red, blue or purple, and cyclamens are all shade-loving bulbs, while daffodils and freesias enjoy semi-shade conditions.

Begonias, impatiens, primula and primrose are among the few annuals that thrive in the shade.

THE WINDSWEPT GARDEN

To create a successful garden under harsh and exposed conditions takes patience and a methodical approach. Many people who live near the sea must contend with strong, salt-laden winds that can prove destructive. Others are exposed to inland winds that are bitingly cold.

Many people who put up walls to counteract the vicious elements often find that while walls might afford some protection in their immediate vicinity, they can actually exacerbate the situation by creating what are known as 'wind traps'.

We cannot completely stop the wind but we can reduce its power, and to this end it is more effective to use a fence with open slats, or hedges. If the fence or hedge has an angle or slope – such as a sand dune has – on the windward side, then as the wind strikes it, it would be forced in an upward trajectory and so be much reduced in strength when returning to the ground. This can also be achieved by using a series of wind-resistant plants that rise up in tiers: the first tier should be a flat-growing ground cover, leading onto small shrubs and the highest tier should be a tall, tough, wind-resistant shrub, creating a filtered trajectory. The best plants to use to combat harsh windy conditions would be those that are indigenous to your area.

The main damage caused by wind is that plants dehydrate, as the roots are unable to draw up water fast enough, and so they begin to dry and scorch, and wilt. If the soil is kept moist the plants stand a better chance. To help preserve moisture in seaside soils, plenty of compost should be mixed into the soil when planting, and the surface of the soil should be kept continually covered with compost, or any other suitable mulching material. This not only helps to retain moisture, but keeps the soil cool and prevents the granules of sand from scouring the plants when the wind blows.

If your garden is new, it could take three to four years before you can put in the plants that you love the most. In the first year only the hardiest of plants should be planted, and these should be placed strategically to break the wind and so later create some protected pockets for the more delicate varieties of plants.

When the site is exposed it is better to use younger plants as these will adapt quicker than a fully matured plant would. Remember that plants from nurseries, even tough ones such a rosemary, have been kept under pampered conditions and have not felt the brunt of a howling gale. This means they must be nurtured during their first few weeks until they are established. The stronger the root system of your plants the more easily they can cope with wind, and in the first season they should be fed regularly with food high in phosphates to encourage this. When planting, you could line the holes with a few layers of newspaper to hold in the moisture. This will later decompose and become food for the plant.

Remember that salt often blocks up the pores of plants and this renders them incapable of breathing and sweating, so they greatly appreciate being washed off from time to time, especially during windy spells.

Contrary to the norm, it is often best to overplant in an exposed garden as this helps the plants to protect and support one another.

TOUGH, LOW-GROWING INDIGENOUS WILDFLOWERS GROW EASILY IN A HARSH CLIMATE AND ARE LESS SUSCEPTIBLE TO STRONG WINDS.

4 CREATING A GARDEN IN A PAVED AREA

Patios, courtyards, rooftops and balconies are usually paved areas. They present something of a design challenge because layout is dictated by the strong geometric shapes of such confined areas, but the fact that most gardening in paved areas is done in containers, which are moveable, makes it a little easier (refer to the Plant List on pages 116–123 to identify plants that are suitable for containers).

In these areas the major challenge is to find a combination of plants that not only thrive but look good as a collective composition (refer to Low-maintenance areas in the Plant List on page 121 for ideas), and to this end it is important to be very well acquainted with all the micro-climates of your paved area – through all the seasons – in order to ensure success.

When designing a garden in a paved area, mistakes are more difficult to conceal and the balance between mass and space becomes critical: objects such as furniture should be related in scale to the height of the surrounding boundaries, and every facet you employ will assume huge importance in the overall effect of the composition.

THE PATIO GARDEN

A patio is an open room, usually adjoining a house, and is often paved and used for outdoor activities. It is not to be confused with an enclosed courtyard, which is surrounded by walls or buildings, although some aspects relating to garden design may be similar.

Most homes today have an outdoor area, usually paved, that is used for entertainment and leisure purposes. Patios commonly flow directly from a room in the house, but can also be incorporated as an independent structure in the larger garden. As the more common option is attached to the house, this is the one with which we will deal.

Ideally, the patio floor should either blend in with the adjoining room, or with the other paved areas of the garden, and should be

slightly sloped away from the house in order to prevent the accumulation of puddles of water.

If you opt for making the paving compatible with the garden, try to carry through the theme of the attached room by using similar containers or furniture. Alternatively, the theme of the patio could be in complete contrast to that of the house, but this must be done in such fashion that the one enhances the other.

Because the patio is usually paved, you are more likely to grow most of your plants in containers and/or in hanging baskets. Avoid cluttering the patio with too many pots or troughs.

A SHADY TREE, OVERLOOKING A GRAVEL AREA WITH STRATEGICALLY PLACED POTS AND AN INTRIGUING STATUE, PROVIDES THE SETTING FOR AN ENTERTAINMENT AREA.

If the patio is positioned to receive the midday sun, some sort of shading device should be erected – perhaps an awning, or a pergola covered with a deciduous creeper that will ensure cool, leafy shade in summer, but allow winter sun to penetrate when it loses its leaves. A patio often creates a warm micro-climate, and so you may well be able to grow more tender plants than would be the case in a more 'open' garden. Shrubs with neat, upright shapes are well suited to patios.

If your patio receives four to five hours of sunlight a day, you can plant sun-loving plants, but if the area receives less than this, you would need to plant shade-loving plants. If you have both sunny and shady spots, you could accumulate an interesting variety of plants. Remember to keep plants with similar requirements together – making them easier to maintain. A low wall surrounding a patio

can have container plants on top of it, or even be used as a wall box, either way creating another level.

Climbing plants can be encouraged to grow up the walls or support beams or pillars using trellises.

CREATING A GARDEN IN A PAVED AREA

THE COURTYARD GARDEN

Specifically designed as an 'outdoor room', a courtyard – or any area surrounded by walls – should reflect a cool and calm atmosphere.

As the courtyard is completely or partially surrounded by the house, it is essential to carry through some of the dominant style of your home – particularly of the room or rooms that lead onto the courtyard or through which the courtyard is visible.

This can be accomplished with simple touches, such as using one of your outdoor chairs inside the room that leads outside, or by duplicating the style of a pot or container, or even a plant, inside and out.

If the floor tiles used inside could be used in the garden, the effect would be dramatic and appealing, and extend your home into the outdoors with little further effort.

Because the courtyard garden is a confined space, it is better to use a few large pots rather than many small ones. A lot of tiny pots gathered together tend to create a busy atmosphere,

and become the focal point of the courtyard, destroying the illusion of space.

Scented plants are often most effective in enclosed areas because the perfume is partially 'trapped'.

In addition to containers, raised beds can be planted to create a visual unification with the house. They also provide a vertical pattern.

The garden will be visible throughout the year from the house, as many of the indoor rooms will overlook the courtyard, so emphasis should be on plants that remain appealing all year long. These permanent plants should form the framework or skeleton of your design, and space may

HERE A COURTYARD BECOMES A TRANSITIONAL SPACE BETWEEN THE HOUSE AND THE WORLD OUTSIDE. THE VERTICAL SHAPES OF THE CYPRESS TREES, JUXTAPOSED AGAINST TERRACOTTA WALLS, CREATE A REFLECTIVE AND HARMONIOUS AREA.

be left for seasonal annuals and perennials. However, it is important not to overuse colour, as it tends to dramatically enliven the area that is meant to be calming.

Remember that in a small area, any tree you plant will alter the amount of sunlight received in the garden as it matures. If you clear a bed inbetween the tiles or paving to plant a tree in the ground rather than in a pot, remember that trees with strong surface roots are likely to lift paving, so try to stay away from these.

A courtyard garden that is used at night can be greatly enhanced with strategically placed lighting. Ornamental lights can add drama and magic to a garden, and you should wait until dark before deciding where such lights should be placed, preferably when the garden is nearing maturity so that the lights are not obscured with the passage of time. Also, the perfume of flowers is most intense in the evening.

When you choose furniture for your courtyard, try to carry through something of the style you have in the room overlooking the garden. For example, use a colour that is reflected boldly indoors. Say you have a large rug that is mostly olive-green – you could cover the cushions of the outdoor chairs in the same colour fabric, enhancing the feeling of the courtyard being part of the house.

TOPIARIED STANDARDS WITH THEIR 'LOLLIPOP-SHAPED' HEADS ARE ARRANGED WITH GEOMETRIC PRECISION IN THIS COURTYARD. THE EFFECT IS STYLISH, WHILE THE ROSES PLANTED BENEATH THE TREES AND THE GRASS GROWN BETWEEN THE PAVERS PULLS THE FORMAL DESIGN TOGETHER.

THE BALCONY GARDEN

Most balconies are outside, open rooms that lead off another room or a flat. They can be several metres above the ground with no groundfloor garden in sight. In cases where the balcony overlooks a garden, it should complement the general style or theme of the garden, and so become one of the rooms within the *garden*, rather than an extension of the house.

Balconies of flats, on the other hand, *are* an extension of the home and so should be laid out first as a room – accommodating traffic, ornaments and furniture, perhaps even a clotheshorse, albeit occasionally, and storage space – and only then as a garden, when spaces can be filled with container plants.

Unfortunately, the average balcony has a fickle climate, making it extremely challenging to obtain the particular style and effect you may want from your plants. The elements influencing a balcony garden can be downright hostile, from freezing cold to scorchingly hot, and often as not exposed to the wind. To make matters worse, balconies usually have a ceiling, and this can effectively reverse the seasons by keeping most of the direct sun out during summer when the sun is directly above, and allowing plenty of sun during winter when the trajectory of the sun is at a lower angle.

Wind and total shade make for the worst combination, as most shade-loving plants are of a gentle disposition, and usually enjoy the protection of a forest or jungle in their natural habitat, and the real toughies of the plant world are often the least popular.

People who have a balcony for a garden sometimes persist with remarkable tenacity in their attempts to grow 'soft' favourites, such as roses. Because the seasons are inexorably altered on most balconies, they are seldom successful.

As you can see, there are more than a few permutations that make the

horticultural side of things a little trying for those who endeavour to garden under these circumstances.

However, don't be discouraged: there is hope – as long as you obey a few simple rules.

As applies to all confined spaces, two or three large plant containers are better than 11 small ones, which would obscure one another, fall over in the wind, stunt the plants and create a feeling of clutter. The soil in small containers also dries out rapidly, enforcing endless bouts of watering and feeding. The principal of 'less is more' also applies to features or statues: one or two bold objects are better than a host of miniature ones, and create a feeling of spaciousness.

Because the balcony is not a room in the garden but rather a garden in a room, the containers and plants should primarily be chosen to complement the furnishings, floor and walls of the balcony and flat.

The containers used should be attractive, as they are one of the main features of the balcony. Unattractive containers can be hidden by planting ivy, or a similar plant that will trail over the edges.

Container sizes may vary, but a 90 x 90 cm pot can support a climbing plant for a wall, or a small tree, which would be semi-bonsaied, three or four small shrubs, two perennials and even a couple of annuals: an entire garden in itself, and one that would provide year-round interest and charm. For a more simplistic approach you could use a single specimen plant and underline it by arranging ornamental stone or planting ground cover around its base.

Other suitable plants for the balcony garden would include tough plants that are strong in form and texture, with a disciplined growth habit, or plants that can be topiaried or made into miniature standards. These types of plants will provide permanent, living features,

A SIMPLE WHITE-PAINTED TRELLIS ENCLOSES THIS BALCONY AND CREATES A TERRACE ATMOSPHERE. EASILY MAINTAINED PLANTS, SUCH AS EVERGREEN IVY IN A HANGING BASKET AND MONDO GRASS IN A TERRACOTTA POT, COMPLETE THE LOOK.

at the same time enlivening the balcony without taking up too much space.

In really extreme situations it pays to over-plant the containers slightly as the plants offer one another a certain amount of support and protection, sort of holding one another up, and by trapping the air between them they keep their immediate environment a bit warmer. When you do overplant, bear in mind that regular clipping and shaping would be necessary to keep the plants from smothering each other.

Indulging in a seasonal garden by planting out annuals and perennials and bulbs every season for a short, sharp three- to four-month burst of colour can be fun, at the same time allowing you to play with different plant and colour combinations, but you would have to survive a forlorn and bleak winter period. To this end it is wise to follow the farmers' method of crop

rotation, particularly to help prevent diseases – unless you intend to make use of completely fresh soil every year. However, the seasonal garden is often the best way to go when there is only a window period of good weather in an otherwise hostile environment.

Another problem that besets most balconies is the tendency for plants to grow towards the light, leaving you with a lot of horizontal greenery or with the flowers all facing away from you. Containers should be turned every two or three weeks during the period of strongest light, and to this end containers that have a wheel base would be especially useful.

Remember this: the smaller the area, the more impact each object has on the overall scheme of things, so a mistake in the design, whether it is one unattractive pot or one bedraggled plant, can become the focal point of your balcony.

A SHADED BALCONY
GARDEN FILLED WITH
LUSH GREEN FOLIAGE
INTERSPERSED WITH
BRIGHTLY COLOURED
IMPATIENS.

THE ROOFTOP GARDEN

A rooftop garden provides a wonderful feeling of freedom, especially if you spend your working days in an enclosed environment. Relaxing in a rooftop garden can make you feel as if you are on top of the world, and the elevated position makes for a unique outdoor atmosphere.

However, there are many factors to be taken into consideration when planning a rooftop garden. Rooftop floors usually leave much to be desired, but their biggest problem is that they are not usually designed to sustain much weight. So, unless you have the money for structural reinforcements, you should choose a light flooring. The surface must also allow for drainage. Ornamental crushed stone, a wooden deck, thin, grouted tiles or all of them combined make for the lightest solutions, after paint. An engineer may need to be consulted when installing a floor, particularly if you plan to install raised planters or large containers. In any event, it would be best to check with an expert.

As with all geometrically-shaped small gardens, the surface pattern and the placing of three-dimensional objects within that pattern, is of utmost importance. There must be a balance between space and mass within the framework of the ground pattern and the textural combinations should be pleasing.

Opposite: HERE A ROOFTOP HAS BEEN TRANSFORMED INTO AN OASIS BY USING ONLY GREEN FOLIAGE. THE VELVET TEXTURE OF THE ORNAMENTAL GRASS PATCHES SOFTENS THE CONCRETE SURROUNDS. Left: STANDARD ICEBERG ROSES HAVE BEEN UNDERPLANTED WITH A MIXTURE OF ANNUALS AND PERENNIALS; THE EFFECT MAKES IT HARD TO BELIEVE THAT YOU ARE ON A ROOFTOP, RATHER THAN IN A GROUNDFLOOR GARDEN!

The conditions on most rooftops are more extreme than those at ground level, and it pays to use strong plants that can tolerate the prevailing conditions. Wind is usually the biggest contender, and a double-wall planter (a trough made by building a wall in front of the parapet to create a plant box) on the periphery, with strong screening plants is one way of protecting the area. A strong trellis wall with container-grown climbing plants, or self-supporting ivies is another. These would in any event soften the environment without taking up too much space. While a glass wall will protect you from the wind and allow you a magnificent view, the sunlight will most likely be magnified and so scorch your plants.

Some shade would be necessary too, and while a small tree would seem to be the obvious answer, think about the fact that it would need a container at least one square metre in size, and, when wet, would weigh as much as two tons!

An aluminium pergola with wooden crossbeams that could be overgrown with climbers would be the more logical choice. This would not only reduce the glare, and provide privacy and shelter, but it could also incorporate a built-in seating arrangement.

Rooftop gardens usually consist entirely of container plants, so they require frequent feeding. Make sure that water is near at hand and easy to administer. Most of the plants you choose for a roof garden should be tough shrubs that can live for years on end in a container, with as little maintenance as possible.

Most of the tougher shrubs have either a hairy or furry leaf surface, hard, glossy leaves, a waxy layer, or tend to be small-leaved. When grouping these tough specimens, careful consideration should be given to arrangement according to texture and form, making sure that the plants bring out the best in one another.

THE COMBINATION OF FLOWERING AND FOLIAGE PLANTS GIVES THE ILLUSION OF A VAST GARDEN. CREEPERS COVER WALLS AND A TREE PROVIDES SHADE — A CLEVER ACHIEVEMENT ON A ROOFTOP!

CONTAINER GARDENING

Hundreds of millions of plants around the world live in containers, and at least half of them are unhappy with the care and treatment they receive. They live in clay pots, metal bathtubs, wooden wine barrels, plastic liners, copper watering cans, asbestos or concrete containers and innumerable other homes. Indeed without containers some people would have no garden at all.

The truth is that container gardening requires a fair amount of maintenance, somewhat like pets, and should not be indulged in if this care and attention cannot be sustained.

Most shrubs, trees, and other plants will live happily for many years in a good container, under the right conditions and with proper care and attention. It's easy to achieve when you know how, but difficult to impossible if you do not adhere to certain basics.

One of the main problems is that the soil in containers is largely cut off from the natural environment and is therefore in danger of dying unless adequate precautions are taken. If the micro-organisms and earthworms die then you will have real problems trying to resuscitate the soil. Its difficult to add organic material once the plant's roots are established, and this means we must indulge in regular organic feeding.

Soil is meant to breathe and if the container has bad drainage, or is made of non-permeable materials the soil will soon suffocate. Soil that is too heavy becomes compact, forcing out the air. Poor drainage causes the soil to turn into mud at the base of the pot and this heavy concentration of water expels the vital oxygen, which keeps the organisms in the soil alive and active. This mud becomes noxious and the roots, earthworms and micro-organisms die in the resulting airless environment. The rot then seeps upward and poisons the remainder of the soil in the container and so the plants sicken and often die.

At this stage it is pointless to poison the insects and fungi that attack the plant, as the plant's resistance to disease is almost non-existent, and pests will keep returning until the plant dies. Watering the plant will only aggravate the situation; so the best option is to remedy the soil condition and try to restore the plants' immune system. This is done by removing the toxic soil and replacing it with good soil. Water the plant sparingly, and *then* attack the pests. As the plant recovers so will its immune system.

Plants in long, narrow pots with a small surface area exposed to the air are in danger of poisoning at the base, especially when there are insufficient drainage holes to remove the water trapped at the base of the pot. The danger of over-watering is usually at its greatest when the plants are newly planted, because most of the water slips by the undeveloped roots and accumulates below. At this early stage, regular light watering, sometimes twice a day in a hot spot, is preferred to heavy watering at longer intervals. Trays under container plants can lead to waterlogging, and containers on paved surfaces should rather be raised slightly off the surface for good drainage.

When the plant or plants are mature and the root system takes up the entire pot then the problem becomes the opposite. Now you become a slave to regular watering if you want really healthy plants. Either it is time to replant or to accept the routine of regular watering and feeding.

Alternately, shallow pots with wide surfaces are prone to drying out, and it can become almost impossible to keep them constantly moist. Incessant watering strips the soil of its nutrients and essentially it is a balance between these two extremes that we need to achieve.

If you have a container garden it is imperative to have a watering system close at hand to alleviate the endless lugging of cans and buckets to your garden. Miss a beat and you have problems. Not all plants communicate their thirst to us by wilting. Your rosemary bush can stand in bone-dry soil for days without showing signs of stress, and then you water it and only two days later half the leaves go yellow, leaving you mystified because now the soil is moist. A moisture meter is very helpful in these cases

because techniques such as sticking your finger in the soil or tapping the pot take years to perfect, and even then one can be deceived.

Soil in containers is not able to regenerate itself and it is by regular feeding at the right times that you maintain healthy plants.

Containers can become a feature when placed in an incidental fashion – in a bed of plants or in water – even with no plants in them, and can replace a sculpture as the focal point.

Finding the right spot for your pot may entail lugging the container around the garden until it looks perfect; and you can say quite rightly that the pot has chosen its own home.

THE RANDOM PLANTING OF DAISIES IN THIS SCATTER OF CLAY POTS IS SIMPLE AND ATTRACTIVE. TOO MANY PLANTS WOULD HAVE SPOILED THE EFFECT OF SIMPLICITY.

Suspended or Vertical Planting

In some small gardens there are narrow, confined spaces that may be paved, possibly with pipes running beneath the ground, and these areas have no room for planting in any form.

These awkward, usually unpleasant-looking places could be prettily clothed in cascading or trailing plants that have been planted in suspended containers.

Small, ornate pots are not ideal for these areas and in any event are almost impossible to maintain.

However, many of today's retaining walls are made from hollow concrete bricks filled with soil, and these form a perfect support for plants used to create a vertical garden. You could

A DIFFICULT INCLINE BECOMES A VERTICAL GARDEN OF ASSORTED PLANTS. THESE HOLLOW RETAINING BLOCKS PRESENT ENDLESS POSSIBILITIES FOR PLANT COMBINATIONS, TURNING POTENTIAL PROBLEM AREAS INTO SHOWPIECES.

either plant up these containers and blocks with climbers or creepers that would eventually completely obscure the wall, or you could compose a garden with a variety of plants, predominantly the types that cascade downward.

In suspended containers or hollow brick walls, you could combine small plants that stand upright, with cascading types, taking care not to put cascading types directly above the upright plants otherwise they will be smothered.

Because of the confined growing space we must use small-growing shrubs that will never want for more root space, or long-lasting perennials that need only be changed every four or five years, as it can be quite a task to remove the old plants and soil and replant afresh.

The trap most gardeners fall into with suspended planting is to make use of too many varieties of plant. This can look pretty to begin with but inevitably the plants get tangled up and start to swamp one another, necessitating endless clipping to retain a vestige of respectability. While this approach works well with annuals, it seldom applies to perrenials and shrubs as they tend to grow at different speeds and end up crushing one another.

If you prefer an informal flowering mix, then arrange the plants in groups of three, five or seven, so that each grouping retains its identity in the scheme of things. Apart from being more attractive, this arrangement is much easier to maintain.

Larger groups or sweeps of the same plant make for a neater, calmer composition than a multitude of haphazard individuals, and these sweeps can be arranged in a number of interesting patterns.

Plants that grow upright – such as the ornamental grass family – provide us with a number of interesting and attractive options from which to choose. Ornamental grasses come in a wide range of foliage colour and heights and make good colour contrasts. There are a number of upright perennials with sword-shaped leaves, many of which bear attractive flowers.

Ground covers are inclined to weep or cascade and so are suitable for suspended planting. A number of herbs too are very happy to be in a position where they can hang, and these include oregano, thyme and mint.

Suspended gardens are best fed with a liquid fertilizer as these are easy to use, and are much less likely to burn than granular fertilizers.

The window-box garden

When your garden consists only of one or two window boxes, then these humble troughs can assume major importance in the life of the owner. It is a wonderful sight when a number of window-box gardeners live adjacent to one another, for the sight from the street of rows of window boxes filled with bright blooms is delightful.

Remember that a window box will be viewed from both inside the house and from the outside so there should be some link in terms of colour. You will want to be able to open the window, or at least see out of it, and so it is the low-growing and trailing plants that are best suited to window boxes, as these do not need much root space, nor do they grow too tall. Permanent shrubs are seldom used because of the

shallow root space available, and because they soon become root bound or too large. Succulents can live for many years without becoming root bound or oversized, making them a good choice for a sunny window box.

Low-growing annuals, such as lobelia, alyssum, bush sweet peas, nasturtiums and annual pinks are all very rewarding in the confines of a trough.

In cold climates window-box gardeners tend to plant not only annuals but also perennials on a seasonal basis, and they only indulge in these gardening activities

TWO SIMPLE WINDOW BOXES FILLED WITH GERANIUMS OF ONE COLOUR PROVDE A DRAMATIC AND EYE-CATCHING EFFECT FOR PASSERS-BY.

during summer, whereas those in gentler climes can grow winter annuals, and have fun choosing a new theme twice a year. These lucky people can use violas, pansies, and primulas, amongst others. A window box that receives plenty of sunshine makes fertile territory for low-growing herbs such as marjoram, thyme, sage, basil, parsley and chives, and can be especially useful when suspended beneath the kitchen window. A herb box has the added advantage of repelling flies.

There are some perennials and small shrubs that can live for two to three years in a small box as long as they have the benefit of regular feeding during the growing season. Here we look to the small-growing agapanthus, miniature roses, and the smaller members of the Veronica family, which only require the odd snip here and there. As there are many new dwarf varieties being introduced onto the market, all the time, keep a look-out at your local nursery.

Many bulbs do very well in window boxes as they find the depth of the average window box to their liking, and here they are safe from the moles. In strong sunlight, you can make use of ranunculas, scented freesias, narcissi, among others, while in the semi-shade hyacinths and cyclamens do well.

THE BANKING OF A NUMBER OF CONTAINERS SUCCESSFULLY CREATES THE EFFECT OF A FLOWERBED. AS THE PLANTS TRAIL AND LINK TOGETHER, THE STARKNESS OF THE CONTAINERS IS SOON CONCEALED.

Hanging baskets

Hanging baskets are far better suited to small gardens than large ones, where they would be lost in a crowd of other plants. A basket garden can make a small area appear larger, can be used to soften upright poles, or be suspended from a balcony roof or the beam of a pergola, and bring beauty and colour to otherwise dead spaces.

Due to the limited size of most hanging baskets, and the regular maintenance required, most gardeners prefer to use the hanging basket as a seasonal addition to the summer garden, and therefore there is a tendency to use annuals and ground covers.

Because hanging baskets dry out so rapidly when exposed, even with plastic liners and water-retentive acid compost as a mix, it is best to position them where they get little wind and not more than a half-day's sun in hot climates. Granules that retain water and slow-release foods are available nowadays, and these cut out lots of the maintenance. The larger the container, the easier it is to keep it moist, and it's worth remembering

that it is virtually impossible to over-water a hanging basket, but it is very easy to starve it. Hanging-basket gardens need lots of regular feeding to keep the plants in good condition.

Like any garden, a hanging basket can be planted in a number of styles, but for many years it has been fashionable to use a number of different but compatible plants together, rather than just one plant.

Cascading plants such as the ivy geraniums, lobelia, helichrysum, bellflower and nasturtiums are popular as they hide the basket more readily than plants with a rigid growth habit, such as begonias. Impatiens, vinca and spurflowers all fare well in hanging baskets in shady areas.

In recent years a number of new, hybridised perennials – such as perennial petunias and snapdragons – have

become available. These cascading-type plants have been specifically produced with the hanging-basket market in mind.

5 GARDEN STYLES

While modern gardens can be laid out in a number of ways, there are still two main design styles, namely formal and informal. In a simplified form the formal style is once again becoming popular as it is well suited to small gardens. The main reason for this swing to the garden style of old is that it requires relatively little maintenance. However, the style depends entirely on symmetrical, well-balanced lines and plant groups.

The informal-style garden arose in direct contrast to the over-ornate and often ostentacious formal garden. Gardeners began to seek a more 'natural' look – one with flowing curves, and a more random growth of plant material. The informal style is very adaptable, and there are many variations of it. The most popular themes include the tropical, low-maintenance and Mediterranean gardens. These styles are basically Western in origin, while the Japanese garden has evolved according to Eastern ideas and religious traditions.

Plants suited to each of the specific garden styles mentioned on the following pages can be found on pages 119–123 of this book.

THE MODERN FORMAL GARDEN

To be successful any garden design should blend in with the architecture of the house. This is especially true with regard to the formal design, which should only be used with the straight, well-balanced lines of Georgian- or Regency-style houses. This more classical architectural style is widely used in modern cluster-house developments, and so more and more people are using a formal layout in their gardens, to blend in with the style of the house.

The formal design is incorporated in the two components that make up the garden, i.e. hard surfaces such as stone or brick paving, statues, pools, fountains, benches and archways, and soft surfaces comprising all plant material.

Neat, clipped hedges are used to define beds that are laid out in geometric shapes. In a formal garden, unlike in an informal one, all the lines of beds and pathways are straight and not curved. A fountain in the middle of the garden would form a centrepiece with straight-lined beds radiating outwards. The lines would lead the eye to this main feature as well as to strategically placed statues, urns and containers. These should be bold, with their scale relating to the house rather than to the low hedges. The style of all the features must also suit the house. Only old-fashioned, classical shapes and designs should be used. While almost any plants can be used, the emphasis should be on those that have small leaves and a neat growth habit, especially those that are going to be clipped as hedges or topiary.

Traditional plants that are found in a formal garden include box, myrtle and various conifers.

THE LINES OF THIS GARDEN ARE ARCHITECTURAL AND ORDERED. BRICK, GRAVEL AND A SIMPLE TWO-TONE COLOUR SCHEME OF GREENS AND WHITES MODERNIZE THIS FORMAL GARDEN.

THERE IS SO MUCH TO
LOOK AT IN THIS SMALL
SQUARE GARDEN. THE
PEBBLES — SCATTERED IN
FORMAL, GEOMETRIC
STYLE — COMPLEMENT
THE ORNAMENTAL
STATUES THAT FORM THE
FOCAL POINT OF THE
GARDEN, AND AT THE
SAME TIME PROVIDE A
STARK AND INTERESTING
TEXTURAL AND COLOUR
CONTRAST WITH THE
SURROUNDING FOLIAGE.

THE COTTAGE GARDEN

The cottage garden's origins lie in the type of garden that developed around the cottages of the people who lived and worked on the large estates of the nobility during the 17th and 18th centuries. Each cottager was allowed a small tract of land around his cottage, which was primarily used to meet the fresh fruit and vegetable requirements of the household. Most cottagers would also keep pigs and chickens. In this purely functional garden, any open spaces around the cottage would be cobbled or covered with stone chips or sea shells, and the same material would be used for pathways.

While to begin with this was a strictly functional style with no set layout, colourful flowers, especially perennials, were increasingly used, which gave the cottage garden its distinctive look. During the latter part of the 18th and 19th century, the cottage garden fell from favour as being too 'rustic'.

But with the move away from a formal layout in more modern times, the cottage theme was once again seen as an attractive and romantic design, and, with its extensive use of perennials and self-seeding annuals, its lack of lawns and clipped hedges, and its essentially low maintenance, it is well suited to modern life styles.

In a small garden, however, there needs to be a fair amount of control or the garden will quickly become overgrown. The emphasis should be on shrubs and trees to provide a strong framework. Certain features, such as benches, arches and doorways framed by creepers, are also an integral part of a cottage garden, but their style must fit in with the cottage look, and must be old-fashioned rather than modern.

A TUMBLE OF ROSES, LAVATERA AND ASSORTED PERENNIALS MAKES THIS COTTAGE GARDEN A HAPHAZARD DELIGHT. CLIMBING ROSES AND A FOUNTAIN ADD TO ITS CHARM.

The layout of the cottage garden is almost casual. Paths, for example, wander in and out, and if a clump of perennials develops in the pathway, then the path simply continues around it. The only fixed pathway is the one that runs from the front door to the boundary gate. This unusually straight pathway is most symbolic of a cottage-style garden, and would typically have an arched gate and front door at either end, both clothed in climbing roses.

There is a wide range of plants that can be used in a cottage garden, but try to concentrate on those that have a soft, pretty look and

Right: A PERFECT EXAMPLE OF THE MAGIC OF A COTTAGE GARDEN. HERE PLANTS SEEM TO HAVE FOUND THEIR OWN HOMES AS SPACE ALLOWED, WHILE A PATH HAS BEEN TRODDEN BETWEEN THE FLOWERS
Opposite: THE CHOICE OF LAVENDER, PLUMBAGO AND ICEBERG ROSES IS VERY EFFECTIVE IN THIS GARDEN. THE ADDITION OF THE BENCH PLACED ON GRAVEL CREATES A UNIFIED DESIGN.

bear plenty of flowers. Traditional cottage garden plants include roses and clematis, perennials such as delphinium, Michaelmas daisy and perennial phlox, and trees like silver birch and flowering cherries.

The cottage garden is an adaptable theme and so where the original 'cottage' plants – especially some of the perennials – cannot be grown due to climatic conditions, you can easily find substitutes. Today most cottage gardens do have small lawn areas but these should be kept to a minimum, and should be edged with suitable ground covers. While a cottage garden looks at its best with the typical low-eved thatch-roofed cottage, it can be used with many other architectural styles, from comtemporary ranch-style homes to the Victorian cottage. It is, however, out of place with ultra-modern and Spanish or Moorish designs.

THE TROPICAL GARDEN

The tropical garden uses almost the opposite plants to those you would use in a cottage garden, as this theme depends on plants with large, decorative foliage and only a few flowers to give it a 'jungle' feel. Although all true tropical and sub-tropical plants need moist, warm, frost-free growing conditions, there is still a wide range of suitable plants that can be used in cooler regions to create the same feel. Besides that, temperatures in smaller, enclosed areas are often much warmer than those in more open gardens, making it possible to grow plants that are suitable to a climate other than that in which you live.

The backbone of your tropical garden should be some tall plants such as palms, bamboo or tree ferns. Below them you should use lower-growing foliage shrubs interspersed with clumps of large-leafed perennials, while the walls should be bedecked with lush, fast-growing creepers. The 'floor' of your jungle garden should be covered with various ground covers as there is no place for lawn in these conditions. The plants should be close together to give the impression that they are competing with one another.

Where you need a flat, open area for entertaining you should use brick paving or bark chips. Soft round stones, bricks or wood chips should also be used for pathways.

Water is an integral part of a tropical garden, and this should be incorporated in the form of a still pond with fish and water lilies, fringed by ground covers and ferns, a softly trickling streamlet or a gentle waterfall.

A wooden log bench should be situated in a place

DEEP GREEN FOLIAGE GIVES A SENSE OF MYSTERY TO THIS TROPICAL GARDEN. KHOI FISH SWIM UNDISTURBED BENEATH AN OVERHANG OF FUCHSIAS. THE EFFECT IS LUSH AND TRANQUIL.

where you can benefit fully from the advantages of this quiet retreat.

Although permanent plants are used, you will still need to do a fair amount of maintenance to keep the jungle under control, as while you want to have the garden full of plant growth, you must still be able to move around.

While this style can be used with almost any type of architecture, it tends to go best with modern designs, where high, blank walls can help off set the tall clumps of palms or trees grown as features.

Right: THE STRATEGIC PLACING OF THIS WATER FEATURE CREATES A DAMP ENVIRONMENT IN WHICH ABUNDANT FOLIAGE PLANTS, LIKE FERNS, CAN FLOURISH.

Opposite: DEEP-GREEN TREE FERNS AND TALL-STEMMED PALMS HAVE BEEN CLEVERLY POSITIONED IN THIS SMALL SPACE TO RECREATE THE AMBIENCE THAT IS NATURAL IN THE LUSH DENSITY OF A JUNGLE.

THE LOW-MAINTENANCE GARDEN

Lifestyles have changed considerably in recent times. People who work a full day do not have much time to spend on their gardens, yet still want an attractive garden in which they can relax. This need has given rise to a garden style whose principal aim is to look interesting and colourful throughout the year, but which requires as little maintenance as possible.

Once again, planning is of utmost importance, for this style can rapidly become dull and dreary. Particular attention must be paid to the basic principles of design so that the garden has a good overall structure, rhythm and balance. As the layout of the garden is informal, care must be taken to ensure that the curves of the beds are generous so that where there is lawn this is easy to mow. To cut down on maintaining lawn edges, a hard edge such as brick or concrete should be used. Lawns, which need a great deal of care, should be restricted and open areas should either be paved or covered with tough, easy-to-grow ground covers.

In this type of garden, the type of plants used and their placement plays a vital role. The main criteria for the plants is that they must be easy to grow, have a neat growth habit so that they don't need constant clipping back or pruning, and should either have colourful foliage or be free flowering. Shrubs and ground covers will form the main framework, but there are a number of evergreen perennials that can also be used.

For best visual results plant groups of shrubs, especially the lower-growing ones, rather than individual types. As beds of annuals have no place in the low-maintenance garden, extra seasonal colour can be achieved by planting easy-to-grow annuals and bulbs, which can be relatively easily maintained when planted in containers.

While the particular plants that you use will depend to a large extent on your climatic conditions, there are some — specifically conifers — that

can be grown in almost all conditions, and are a top choice for the low-maintenance garden. Not only do they have a neat and tidy growth habit, but they come in a wide variety of shapes and attractive blends of foliage colours. You will also find that plants indigenous to your area or those from other countries with a similar climate are a good choice, as they will not need extra watering or feeding to keep them in good condition.

As watering is extremely time-consuming, a low-maintenance garden should ideally have an irrigation system, preferably of the automatic type.

THE PLANTS USED HERE NEED LITTLE ATTENTION. SCULPTURED ALOE LEAVES COMBINE WITH VARIEGATED *COPROSMA* AND ROSE-LIKE, GREY *ECHEVERIA SECUNDA* WITH DRAMATIC EFFECT.

Another way to cut down on maintenance is to use long-lasting, durable materials for fences, walls, retaining walls, paving and features. These may initially prove to be expensive, but will easily pay for themselves in the long term. The low-maintenance garden style suits almost all types of architecture, but is especially well suited to the more modern homes.

A GARDEN HAS BEEN CREATED ON A DIFFICULT, WINDSWEPT MOUNTAIN SLOPE BY USING TOUGH, EASY-TO-GROW PLANTS. EVENING PRIMROSE PROVIDES A DASH OF VIBRANT YELLOW.

THE MEDITERRANEAN GARDEN

White-washed walls, troughs of brightly coloured annuals, vine-covered pergolas and a softly splashing fountain are the basic features of a design synonymous with the Mediterranean regions of Europe and North Africa. Its origins date back centuries and often appear in the courtyard gardens of Moorish Spain.

Climate is one of the dominant factors shaping this style. In Mediterranean regions the summers are long, hot and dry, while winters are mild, damp and usually frost free. The region is mainly coastal, so it can be very windy, and soil conditions tend to be poor.

The Mediterraean style is very adaptable and so can be used in many areas with similar climatic conditions. Because of the long, hot summers, lawns – which require plenty of water – are kept to a minimum or disregarded altogether. Where open areas are needed, for outdoor living for example, the surface is paved with some sort of suitable material such as bricks, stone slabs, cobbles, pebbles, stone chips or crushed seashells. Tough, low-maintenance ground covers are used to fill in open spaces between shrubs in beds and borders.

Terraces and patios are usually formal in shape, but the layout of beds and containers is abstract. Planting is simplistic, making each plant or group of plants a feature on its own. Plants with strong shape and form, such as aloes, succulents, cacti, yuccas and palms, are good choices as they suit both the architecture and the climate. Bougainvilleas, with their large trusses of vividly coloured flowers, are among the best creepers for covering large expanses of wall, but any creeper suited to your climatic conditions can be used.

BRILLIANT PURPLE AND CERISE WALLS AND TERRACOTTA POTS FILLED WITH FLOWERING SHRUBS AND ANNUALS CREATE AN EVOCATIVE 'GREEK ISLE' FEELING.

To provide extra colour and interest, containers in all shapes and sizes are planted up with shrubs, flowering annuals, perennials and ground covers – window boxes filled with bright red geraniums immediately spring to mind.

While the containers can be rich terracotta in colour they can also be painted in deep blue or striking orange hues. These same vibrant colours are used on gates and window frames so that the garden is linked with the house.

Where there are banks and retaining walls, ground covers help to knit the soil and prevent erosion. Because of the long summers most entertaining is done outdoors, so wide patios are essential in a Mediterranean-style garden.

These should be covered with a pergola draped with a suitable deciduous creeper, traditionally a vine, to allow winter sunlight to shine through.

Frescoes with scenes of sea and beaches, or mountains, are often used to

decorate expanses of wall and provide that special Mediterranean feel.

Water is an integral part of the Mediterranean garden, and can be incorporated in many forms; a central fountain on the patio, or a wall fountain – you could even have a large pond near the living area, complete with fish.

The Mediterranean style is adaptable, but looks best with Moorish- and Spanish-type architecture.

Opposite: DURING THE LONG, HOT SUMMERS OF A MEDITERRANEAN CLIMATE, A COVERED PATIO BECOMES AN ESSENTIAL EXTENSION OF THE HOUSE.
Left: HOT TERRACOTTA WALLS DEFINING A CONFINED PASSAGE AT THE SIDE OF A HOUSE CAN BE CONVERTED TO BECOME A COOL WALKWAY WITH THE CLEVER USE OF EVERGREEN SHRUBS AND NODDING WHITE PANSIES.

THE JAPANESE GARDEN

Unlike the gardens of Western civilizations, Japanese gardens form a vital part of Japan's peoples' religion and culture. There are three main types of Japanese garden, namely the traditional Zen Buddhist garden, the classical stroll garden, and the Tea Garden.

The Zen garden is regarded as a place of sacred communication, where the essence of Nature and Man's being can be captured through quiet meditation. Thus it is a garden to be looked at rather than lived in.

The basic aim of the Zen design is to produce a natural landscape using materials that symbolize the components, rather than using the actual components themselves.

Plants are kept to a minimum. The boundary of the garden is usually an informal hedge of bamboo. A carefully placed spring-flowering tree, such as flowering cherry, can be used to represent the renewal of life. Other plants include conifers, various types of bamboo and ornamental grasses.

The classical stroll garden, while still tranquil, has more movement in it. In Japan space has always been at a premium. Thus, to give the illusion of a larger area, the garden must flow in and out, and lead to one or two central features.

Water, the gift of life, plays a prominent role in garden design. It is often in the form of tiered waterfalls that run over stone or even large sections of bamboo.

This tinkle of water and the soft sounds of wind chimes give this garden a special ethos. The plants used are very subdued with only a splash of colour. Swathes of grass, such as mondo, edge the soft curves of the stroll pathways.

The Japanese Tea Garden became famous through the opera 'Madame Butterfly',

and is essentially a simplified indoor living area, which is kept very neat. It could lead off a stroll pathway or off a sand garden. It is, in essence, a small, totally enclosed paved area where tea and refreshments are consumed.

The furniture is made of glossed cane, and a bamboo hedge gives one total privacy. The entrance to a 'strict' Tea Garden could be marked by a classical stone lantern.

SMALL GARDEN PLANT LIST

spp. = subspecies cvs = cultivars

Visit your local nursery and garden centre to see what is available for your area and for expert advice.

TREES

Acacia baileyana Bailey's wattle

Acacia karroo soetdoring

Acer buergerianum Chinese maple

Acer negundo 'Variegata' box elder

Acer palmatum Japanese maple

Afrocarpus falcata common yellowwood

Betula pendula silver birch

Bolusanthus speciosus
   South African wisteria

Brachylaena discolor coast silver oak

Callistemon viminalis
   weeping bottlebrush

Calpurnia aurea wild laburnum

Cassia fistula golden shower tree

Ceratonia siliqua carob

Cercis siliquastrum Judas tree

Citharexylum quadrangulare fiddlewood

Cornus florida flowering dogwood

Cupressocyparis leylandii cvs

Cupressus macrocarpa cvs

Cussonia paniculata cabbage tree

Dais cotinifolia pompon tree

Diospyros whyteana bladder-nut

Dombeya rotundifolia wild pear

Ficus benjamina weeping fig

Hymnosporum flavum Australian frangipani

Loxostylis alata tenderwood

Malus floribunda common crabapple

Melaleuca linariifolia
   flax-leaved paperbark

Prunus x blireana
   double-pink flowering plum

Prunus cerasifera 'Nigra'
   purple cherry plum

Prunus serrulata Oriental cherry

Rhus pendulina weeping karree

Tabebuia chrysantha yellow tabebuia

Thuja orientalis cvs

Vespris undulata white ironwood

LARGE SHRUBS (2 m+)

Brunfelsia pauciflora 'Eximia'
   yesterday-today-and-tomorrow

Buxus sempervirens common box

Callistemon cvs bottlebrush

Camellia spp. & cvs

Coprosma repens cvs
   mirror plant

Datura cornigera moonflower

Duranta repens golden dewdrop

Duvernoia adhatodoides

Feijoa sellowiana pineapple guava

Gardenia jasminoides

Grewia occidentalis cross-berry

Halleria elliptica wild fuchsia

Hibiscus rosa-sinensis cvs hibiscus

Ilex aquifolium cvs common holly

Ligustrum spp. & cvs privet

Mackaya bella forest bell

Melaleuca spp. & cvs

Murraya exotica orange jessamine

Myrtus communis 'Variegata' myrtle

Nerium oleander cvs oleander

Photinia spp. & cvs Christmas berry

Pittosporum spp. & cvs

Pyracantha spp. & cvs firethorn

Legend: ⛅ sun ◐ semi-shade/shade ✽ flowers 🍂 foliage 🌲 container 〰 wind resistant ● hardy to frost

Robinia hispida rose acacia

Sambucus racemosa
  'Plumosa aurea' golden elder

Schefflera actinophylla
  umbrella-tree

Schefflera arboricola

Syzygium paniculatum brush cherry

Tibouchina spp. & cvs glory bush

Viburnum spp. & cvs

MEDIUM SHRUBS (1–2 m)

Abelia spp. & cvs

Acalypha wilkesiana cvs copperleaf

Allamanda cathartica common allamanda

Anisodontea spp.

Berberis thunbergii cvs

Breynia distacha cvs ice-cream bush

Carissa macrocarpa Natal plum

Chaenomeles speciosa flowering quince

Chamelaucium uncinatum
  Geraldton wax

Codiaeum spp. & cvs

Coleonema spp. & cvs

Escallonia spp. & cvs

Euonymus japonicus cvs

Euryops spp. honey marguerite

Grevillea spp. & cvs

Hydrangea spp. & cvs

Hypoestes aristata ribbon bush

Malaviscus arboreus firedart bush

Nandina domestica heavenly bamboo

Ochna spp. bird's eye bush

Raphiolepis spp. & cvs
  Indian hawthorn

Rhododendron indicum cvs azalea

Rosa cvs roses

Spiraea spp. & cvs spirea

Weigela florida cvs

SMALL SHRUBS AND SUB-SHRUBS (under 1 m)

Agathosma spp. buchu

Ardisia crenata coral berry

Argyranthemum frutescens cvs marguerite daisy

Barleria obtusa cvs bush violet

Berberis thunbergii 'Atropurpurea Nana'
  dwarf berberis

Callistemon cvs
  'Little John' dwarf bottlebrush

Cistus spp. & cvs rock rose

Cuphea spp. & cvs cigarette bush

Diascia spp. & cvs twin spur

Euonymus fortunei

Euonymus japonicus 'Microphyllus'
  dwarf euonymus

Felicia spp. & cvs kingfisher daisy

Fuchsia cvs

Hebe spp. & cvs Veronica

Lavandula spp. & cvs lavender

Melaleuca bracteata
  'Golden Gem' dwarf melaleuca

Pelargonium spp. & cvs
  bush geranium/pelargonium

Pentas lanceolata cvs star-cluster

Punica granatum 'Nana' dwarf pomegranate

Rosmarinus officinalis cvs rosemary

Salvia greggii cvs autumn sage

Serissa foetida 'Variegata' snowflakes

Syzygium paniculatum
  'Globosa' dwarf eugenia

HEDGES (clipped)

Buxus sempervirens common box

Lavandula spp. & cvs lavender

Ligustrum ovalifolium 'Aureum' golden privet

Myrtus communis myrtle

Pittosporum spp. & cvs

Syzygium paniculatum brush cherry

○ semi-hardy   ❁ tender to frost   △ deciduous   ♣ evergreen   ☆ indigenous   ⚡ exotic   † suited to stds (trained as standard)

GROUND COVERS

Aptenia cordifolia — sun, flowers, wind resistant, hardy to frost, ☘, ☆

Arctotis spp. & cvs African daisy — sun, flowers, wind resistant, hardy to frost, ☘, ☆

Campanula spp. & cvs bellflower — sun/semi-shade, flowers, hardy to frost, ☘, ⚡

Convolvulus sabaticus
   ground morning glory — sun/semi-shade, flowers, ○, ☘, ⚡

Dichondra repens wonder lawn — sun/semi-shade, foliage, ○, ☘, ⚡

Duchesnea indica wild strawberry — sun/semi-shade, flowers, hardy to frost, ☘, ⚡

Dymondia margaretae silver carpet — sun, foliage, wind resistant, ○, ☘, ☆

Erigeron karvinskianus — sun, flowers, container, hardy to frost, ☘, ⚡

Geranium incanum carpet geranium — sun, flowers, container, ❄, ☘, ☆

Helichrysum spp. — sun, foliage, container, wind resistant, ○, ☘, ☆

Lamium maculatum cvs — sun/semi-shade, foliage, container, hardy to frost, ☘, ⚡

Lampranthus spp. & cvs vygie — sun, flowers, container, wind resistant, ○, ☘, ☆

Lantana montevidensis
   dwarf mauve lantana — sun, flowers, container, wind resistant, ○, ☘, ⚡

Lysimachia nummularia creeping Jenny — sun, foliage, container, ○, ☘, ⚡

Nepeta cataria catmint — sun/semi-shade, flowers, ☘, ⚡

Pelargonium peltatum ivy geranium — sun, flowers, wind resistant, ○, ☘, ☆

Stachys lanata lamb's ears — sun/semi-shade, foliage, hardy to frost, ☘, ⚡

Sutera spp. — sun/semi-shade, foliage, container, ○, ☘, ☆

Verbena peruviana verbena — sun, flowers, container, wind resistant, ○, ☘, ⚡

Vinca spp. & cvs periwinkle — sun/semi-shade, flowers, container, hardy to frost, ☘, ⚡

Wedelia triternata — sun, flowers, wind resistant, ○, ☘, ⚡

CLIMBERS

Bougainvillea cvs — sun, flowers, container, ○, ☘, ⚡

Clerodendrum splendens
   scarlet clerodendrum — sun/semi-shade, flowers, container, ❄, ☘, ⚡

Ficus pumila tickey creeper — sun/semi-shade, foliage, wind resistant, ○, ☘, ⚡

Gelsemium sempervirens
   Carolina jasmine — sun, foliage, container, ○, ☘, ⚡

Hedera helix cvs English ivy — sun/semi-shade, foliage, hardy to frost, ☘, ⚡

Hibbertia scandens snake vine — sun, flowers, container, ○, ☘, ⚡

Jasminum polyanthum Chinese jasmine — sun, flowers, container, hardy to frost, ☘, ⚡

Lonicera japonica Japanese honeysuckle — sun/semi-shade, flowers, container, hardy to frost, ☘, ⚡

Mandevilla laxa Chilean jasmine — sun/semi-shade, flowers, container, ❄, ☘, ⚡

Mandevilla splendens cvs — semi-shade, flowers, container, ❄, ☘, ⚡

Pandorea jasminoides
   Australian bower plant — semi-shade, flowers, container, ○, ☘, ⚡

Rosa banksiae banksia rose — sun, flowers, container, hardy to frost, △, ⚡

Thunbergia alata black-eyed Susan — sun, flowers, container, ❄, ☘, ☆

Trachelospermum jasminoides
   star jasmine — sun/semi-shade, flowers, container, ○, ☘, ⚡

BULBS/PERENNIALS/GRASSES

NOTE - where available use dwarf cultivars

Achillea mollis cvs yarrow — sun, flowers, hardy to frost, △/☘, ⚡

Acorus gramineus — sun/semi-shade, foliage, ○, ☘, ⚡

Agapanthus spp. & cvs — sun, flowers, wind resistant, ○, ☘, ☆

Anemone hupehensis var *japonica*
   Japanese anemone — sun/semi-shade, flowers, hardy to frost, △, ⚡

Aster novi-belgii cvs Michaelmas daisy — sun, flowers, hardy to frost, △, ⚡

Bergenia cordifolia — sun/semi-shade, flowers, hardy to frost, ☘, ⚡

Bulbinella floribunda cat's tail — sun, flowers, hardy to frost, △, ☆

Carex morrowii — sun/semi-shade, hardy to frost, ☘, ⚡

Clivia miniata — sun/semi-shade, flowers, ○, ☘, ☆

Coreopsis grandiflora — sun, flowers, hardy to frost, ☘, ⚡

Diascia spp. & perennials twin spur — sun, flowers, ○, ☘, ☆

Festuca spp. & cvs — sun, foliage, hardy to frost, ☘, ⚡

Heuchera sanguinea cvs coral bells — sun/semi-shade, flowers, hardy to frost, ☘, ⚡

Lachenalia spp. — sun/semi-shade, flowers, hardy to frost, △, ☆

Leucanthemum maximum cvs — sun, flowers, hardy to frost, ☘, ⚡

Limonium spp. & cvs statice — sun, flowers, wind resistant, hardy to frost, ☘, ⚡

Ophiopogon spp. & cvs mondo grass — sun/semi-shade, foliage, hardy to frost, ☘, ⚡

Penstemon spp. & cvs — sun, flowers, hardy to frost, △, ⚡

Pleioblastus viridistriatus mini bamboo — sun, foliage, hardy to frost, ☘, ⚡

Scabiosa spp. & cvs scabious — sun, flowers, hardy to frost, ☘, ☆

Tulbachia fragrans sweet garlic — sun, flowers, hardy to frost, △, ☆

ANNUALS

Apart from any tall-growing types such as delphiniums and hollyhocks, virtually all seasonal bulbs can be used depending on conditions. This also applies to 'true' bulbs such as *Liliums*, the daffodil family and dutch iris, among others.

☀ sun	◑ semi-shade/shade	❀ flowers	🍃 foliage	🪴 container	≋ wind resistant	● hardy to frost

THE MODERN FORMAL GARDEN

Trees

Note: Trees used in a formal garden need to be selected for their neat, compact growth habit.

Afrocarpus falcata common yellowwood

Cercis siliquastrum Judas tree

Citharexylum quadrangulare fiddlewood

Cupressocyparis leylandii cvs

Cupressus macrocarpa cvs

Dais cotinifolia pompon tree

Ficus benjamina weeping fig

Prunus cerasifera
    'Nigra' purple cherry plum

Thuja orientalis cvs

Large shrubs (2 m+)

Brunfelsia pauciflora 'Eximia'
    yesterday-today-and-tomorrow

Buxus sempervirens common box

Camellia spp. & cvs

Coprosma repens cvs
    mirror plant

Gardenia jasminoides

Ilex aquifolium cvs common holly

Ligustrum spp. & cvs privet

Murraya exotica orange jessamine

Myrtus communis 'Variegata' myrtle

Syzygium paniculatum brush cherry

Thuja orientalis cvs

Thuja occidentalis cvs

Tibouchina spp. & cvs glory bush

Viburnum spp. & cvs

Medium shrubs (1—2 m)

Abelia spp. & cvs

Anisodontea spp.

Carissa macrocarpa Natal plum

Euryops spp. honey marguerite

Escallonia spp. & cvs

Euonymus japonicus cvs

Rahiolepis spp. & cvs
    Indian hawthorn

Rhododendrun indicum cvs azalea

Spiraea spp. & cvs spirea

Small shrubs and sub-shrubs

Ardisia crenata coral berry

Barleria obtusa cvs bush violet

Berberis thunbergii 'Atropurpurea Nana'
    dwarf berberis

Euonymus japonicus 'Microphyllus'
    dwarf euonymus

Euonymus fortunei

Hebe spp. & cvs Veronica

Lavandula spp. & cvs lavender

Pentas lanceolata cvs star-cluster

Punica granatum
    'Nana' dwarf pomegranate

Syzygium paniculatum
    'Globosa' dwarf eugenia

○ semi-hardy ❄ tender to frost △ deciduous ♣ evergreen ☆ indigenous ⚡ exotic † suited to stds (trained as standard)

THE COTTAGE GARDEN

Trees

Acer negundo 'Variegata' box elder ☀ 🍃 ● △ ⚡

Betula pendula silver birch ☀ 🍃 ● △ ⚡

Dais cotinifolia pompon tree ☀ ✿ ○ △ ☆

Hymnosporum flavum Australian frangipani ☀ ✿ ○ ♣ ⚡

Malus floribunda common crabapple ☀ ✿ ● △ ⚡

Prunus spp. & cvs flowering cherry/peach ☀ ✿ ● △ ⚡

Large shrubs (2 m+)

Brunfelsia pauciflora 'Eximia'
  yesterday-today-and-tomorrow ☀/◑ ✿ ♠ ○ ♣ ⚡

Ligustrum spp. & cvs privet ☀ 🍃 ♠ ● ♣ ⚡ †

Myrtus communis myrtle 🍃 ♠ ● ♣ ⚡ †

Photinia spp. & cvs Christmas berry ☀ ✿ 🍃 ♠ ● ♣ ⚡ †

Sambucus racemosa 'Plumosa aurea' golden elder ☀ 🍃 ● △ ⚡

Medium shrubs (1–2 m)

Abelia spp. & cvs ☀ ✿ ♠ ● ♣ ⚡

Berberis thunbergii cvs ☀ 🍃 ♠ ● △ ⚡

Chaenomeles speciosa flowering quince ☀ ✿ ● △ ⚡

Spiraea spp. & cvs spirea ☀ ✿ ● △ ⚡

Weigela floribunda cvs ☀ ✿ ● △ ⚡

Small shrubs

Argyranthemum frutescens cvs marguerite daisy ☀ ✿ ○ ♣ ⚡

Cistus spp. & cvs rock rose ☀ ✿ ≈ ● ⚡

Fuchsia cvs ◑ ✿ ♠ ○ ♣ ⚡ †

Lavandula spp. & cvs lavender ☀ ✿/🍃 ♠ ≈ ○ ♣

Pentas lanceolata cvs star-cluster ☀/◑ ✿ ♠ ❄ ♣ ⚡

Rosmarinus officinalis cvs rosemary ☀ ✿ ♠ ≈ ○ ♣ ⚡

Salvia greggii cvs autumn sage ☀ ✿ ○ ♣ ⚡

Ground covers

Campanula spp. & cvs bellflower ☀/◑ ✿ ● ♣ ⚡

Chrysanthemum paladosum yellow buttons ☀ ✿ ○ ♣ ⚡

Convolvulus sabaticus ground morning glory ☀ ✿ ○ ♣ ⚡

Dianthus spp. & cvs garden pinks ☀ ✿ ● ♣ ⚡

Erigeron karvinskianus ☀ ✿ ● ♣ ⚡

Geranium incanum carpet geranium ☀ ✿ ○ ♣ ⚡

Lamium maculatum cvs ☀/◑ 🍃 ● ♣ ⚡

Nepeta cataria catmint ☀ ✿/🍃 ● ♣ ⚡

Stachys lanata lamb's ears ☀/◑ 🍃 ● ♣ ⚡

Viola spp. & cvs violet ☀/◑ ✿ ● ♣ ⚡

Climbers

Clematis spp. & cvs ☀/◑ ✿ ● ♣ ⚡

Gelsemium sempervirens Carolina jasmine ☀ ✿ ♠ ● ♣ ⚡

Jasminum spp. jasmine ☀ ✿ ♠ ● ♣ ⚡

Lonicera spp. honeysuckle ☀ ✿ ♠ ● ♣ ⚡

Pandorea spp. & cvs ☀ ✿ ♠ ● ♣ ⚡

Rosa banksiae banksia rose ☀ ✿ ♠ ○ ♣ ⚡

Rosa cvs climbing rose ☀ ✿ ♠ ○ ♣ ⚡

Wisteria sinensis Chinese wisteria ☀/◑ ✿ ● △ ⚡

Bulbs/Perennials/Grasses

Achillea spp. & cvs yarrow ☀ ✿ ● △/♣ ⚡

Alstroemeria spp. & cvs Inca lily ☀ ✿ ○ ♣ ⚡

Ammi majus Queen Anne's lace ☀ ✿ ○ △ ⚡

Anemone japonica cvs Japanese anemone ☀/◑ ✿ ● △ ⚡

Aquilegia spp. & cvs columbine ☀/◑ ✿ ● ♣ ⚡

Aster novi-belgii cvs Michaelmas daisy ☀ ✿ ● △ ⚡

Bergenia cordifolia ☀/◑ ✿ ● ♣ ⚡

Campanula spp. & cvs bellflower ☀/◑ ✿ ● ♣ ⚡

Coreopsis spp. & cvs ☀ ✿ ● ♣ ⚡

Erigeron spp. & cvs ☀ ✿ ● ♣ ⚡

Gaillardia aristata blanket flower ☀ ✿ ● ♣ ⚡

Heliotropium peruvianum heliotrope ☀ ✿ ● ♣ ⚡

Leucanthemum maximum cvs ☀ ✿ ● △ ⚡

Penstemon spp. & cvs ☀ ✿ ● △/♣ ⚡

Phlox spp. & cvs phlox ☀ ✿ ● △ ⚡

Physostegia virginiana cvs obedient plant ☀ ✿ ● ♣ ⚡

Scabiosa spp. & cvs scabious ☀ ✿ ● ♣ ⚡

Solidago virgaurea goldenrod ☀ ✿ ● ♣ ⚡

Verbascum spp. & cvs lamb's tail ☀ ✿/🍃 ○ ♣ ⚡

☀ sun   ◑ semi-shade/shade   ✿ flowers   🍃 foliage   ♠ container   ≈ wind resistant   ● hardy to frost

THE TROPICAL GARDEN

Trees/Palms

Chrysalidocarpus lutescens
  golden bamboo

Cussonia spp. cabbage tree

Cyathea spp. tree fern

Datura cornigera moonflower

Schizolobium excelsum feather-duster tree

Syagrus romanzoffianum queen palm

Shrubs

Acalypha spp. & cvs copperleaf

Codiaeum spp. & cvs

Dracaena spp. & cvs dragon palm

Fatsia japonica fatsi

Mussaenda spp. & cvs flag leaf

Perennials/Ferns/Grasses

Alocasia macrorrhiza elephant's ear

Asplenium spp. bird's nest fern

Blechnum spp. dwarf tree fern

Ensete ventricosum ornamental banana

Ophiopogon spp. & cvs mondo grass

Philodendron selloum
  split leaf philodendron

Phormium spp. & cvs flax lily

Plectranthus spp. & cvs spurflower

Strelitzia nicolai wild banana

THE LOW-MAINTENANCE GARDEN

Large shrubs (2 m+)

Agave americana cvs

Agave angustifolia cvs

Nolina recurvata ponytail palm

Cordyline australis cvs

Pandanus baptistii

Yucca aloifolia cvs dagger plant

Medium shrubs (1–2 m)

Adenium obesum 'Multiflorum'

Aloe spp.

Crassula coccinea spp.

Cycas revoluta

Dasylirion longisimum

Echeveria secunda 'Glauca'

Echinocereus pentalophus

Euphorbia caput-medusae spp.

Furcraea foetida cvs

Nopalxochia ackermannii

Small shrubs

Carpobrotus edulis Hottentot fig

Dorotheanthus bellidiformis
  Livingstone daisy

Drosanthemum speciosum

Ferocactus setispinus

Gasteria verrucosa

Glottiphyllum linguiforme

Haworthia pumila

Lampranthus aureus

Mammillaria spp.

Rebutia senilis

○ semi-hardy   ❄ tender to frost   Δ deciduous   ♣ evergreen   ☆ indigenous   ⚡ exotic   † suited to stds (trained as standard)

THE MEDITERRANEAN GARDEN

Trees

Acacia baileyana Bailey's wattle — sun, flowers, semi-shade, hardy to frost

Ceratonia siliqua carob — sun, wind resistant, semi-shade, hardy to frost

Cupressus spp. & cvs cypress — sun, wind resistant, hardy to frost

Ficus rubigonosa rusty fig — sun, wind resistant, semi-shade, hardy to frost

Lagunaria patersonii pyramid tree — sun, wind resistant, semi-shade, hardy to frost

Malaleuca linariifolia flax-leaved paperbark — sun, flowers, wind resistant, semi-shade, hardy to frost

Rhus pendulina karee — sun, wind resistant, semi-shade, container

Large shrubs (2 m+)

Duranta repens golden dewdrop — sun, flowers, semi-shade, hardy to frost

Feijoa sellowiana pineapple guava — sun, flowers, container, wind resistant, hardy to frost

Melaleuca spp. & cvs — sun, flowers/foliage, wind resistant, semi-shade, hardy to frost

Nerium oleander cvs oleander — sun, flowers, container, wind resistant, hardy to frost

Photinia spp. & cvs Christmas berry — sun, flowers/foliage, container, hardy to frost

Medium shrubs (1–2 m)

Abelia spp. & cvs — sun, flowers, container, hardy to frost

Anisodontea spp. — sun, flowers, container, wind resistant, hardy to frost, container

Coleonema spp. & cvs — sun, flowers, wind resistant, hardy to frost, container

Euryops spp. honey marguerite — sun, flowers, wind resistant, hardy to frost, container

Grevillea spp. & cvs — sun, flowers, wind resistant, hardy to frost

Juniperus spp. & cvs juniper — sun, foliage, wind resistant, hardy to frost

Raphiolepis spp. & cvs
  Indian hawthorn — sun, flowers, container, wind resistant, hardy to frost

Small shrubs and sub-shrubs

Agathosma spp. buchu — sun, flowers, container, wind resistant, container

Argyranthemum frutescens cvs
  marguerite daisy — sun, flowers, hardy to frost

Callistemon spp. & cvs bottlebrush — sun, flowers, wind resistant, hardy to frost

Catharanthus roseus
  Madagascar periwinkle — sun, flowers, container, wind resistant, hardy to frost

Centaurea spp. dusty miller — sun, foliage, wind resistant, hardy to frost

Cistus spp. & cvs rock rose — sun, flowers, wind resistant, hardy to frost

Felicia spp. & cvs kingfisher daisy — sun, flowers, wind resistant, container

Hebe spp. & cvs Veronica — sun, flowers, container, wind resistant, hardy to frost

Lavandula spp. & cvs lavender — sun, flowers/foliage, container, wind resistant, hardy to frost

Pelargonium spp. & cvs
  bush geranium/pelargonium — sun, flowers, container, hardy to frost, container

Rosmarinus officinalis cvs rosemary — sun, flowers, container, wind resistant, hardy to frost

Ground covers

Arctotis spp. & cvs African daisy — sun, flowers, container, hardy to frost, container

Aptenia cordifolia — sun/semi-shade, flowers, container, hardy to frost

Convolvulus mauritanicus
  ground morning glory — sun, flowers, container, hardy to frost

Gazania spp. & cvs gazania — sun, flowers, wind resistant, hardy to frost, container

Geranium spp. crane's bill — sun, flowers, container, hardy to frost

Helichrysum spp. — sun, foliage, container, wind resistant, hardy to frost, container

Lampranthus spp. & cvs vygie — sun, flowers, container, hardy to frost, container

Lantana montevidensis
  dwarf mauve lantana — sun, flowers, container, wind resistant, hardy to frost

Osteospermum fruticosum
  creeping daisy — sun, flowers, wind resistant, hardy to frost, container

Pelargonium peltatum ivy geranium — sun, flowers, container, hardy to frost, container

Plectranthus spp. & cvs spurflower — sun, flowers, container, hardy to frost, container

Verbena peruviana creeping verbena — sun, flowers, container, wind resistant, hardy to frost

Climbers

Bougainvillea cvs — sun, flowers, container, hardy to frost, hardy to frost

Distictis buccinatoria Mexican trumpet — sun, flowers, hardy to frost

Senecio tamoides canary creeper — sun, flowers, hardy to frost, container

Thunbergia alata black-eyed Susan — sun, flowers, container, hardy to frost, container

Bulbs/Perennials/Grasses

Agapanthus spp. & cvs — sun, flowers, wind resistant, hardy to frost, container

Bulbinella floribunda cat's tail — sun, flowers, hardy to frost, container

Diascia spp. & cvs twin spur — sun, flowers, hardy to frost, container

Dietes spp. wild iris — sun, flowers, wind resistant, hardy to frost, container

Limonium spp. & cvs statice — sun, flowers, wind resistant, hardy to frost, container

Scabiosa spp. & cvs scabious — sun, flowers, hardy to frost, container

Watsonia spp. — sun, flowers, wind resistant, hardy to frost, container

---

☀ sun ◑ semi-shade/shade ✿ flowers ✐ foliage ⌂ container ≈ wind resistant ● hardy to frost

THE JAPANESE GARDEN

Trees

Acer palmatum Japanese maple	☼/◐	🍃	●	♣	⚡
Cryptomeria japonica	☼/◐	🍃	●	♣	⚡
Prunus spp. & cvs flowering cherry/peach	☼	✽	●	♣	⚡

Shrubs

Chaenomeles speciosa flowering quince	☼	✽	●	♣	⚡
Rhododendron spp. & cvs azalea	☼/◐	✽	○	♣	⚡

Ground covers

Ophiopogon spp. & cvs mondo grass	☼/◐	🍃	○	♣	⚡

Bulbs/Perennials/Grasses

Bambusa spp. & cvs bamboo	☼	🍃	○	♣	⚡
Nandina domestica heavenly bamboo	☼	🍃	○	♣	⚡

○ semi-hardy ✽ tender to frost Δ deciduous ♣ evergreen ☆ indigenous ⚡ exotic † suited to stds (trained as standard)

INDEX TO THE COMMON AND BOTANICAL PLANT NAMES

(Illustrated pages are in *italic* text)

GENERAL INDEX
(Illustrated pages are in *italic* text)